Ann Markham Walsh

Dancing Through Darkness

*When Love and Dreams Survived
a Nazi Death Camp*

Based on the Diary and Recorded Memories
of Selma (Saartje Wijnberg) Engel

Ann Markham Walsh

Brule, Wisconsin

DANCING THROUGH DARKNESS
When Love & Dreams Survived a Nazi Death Camp

Second Edition, Revised

Published by:
Cable Publishing
14090 E Keinenen Rd
Brule, WI 54820
www.cablepublishing.com
E-mail: nan@cablepublishing.com

Based on the Diary and Recorded Memories of Selma (Saartje Wijnberg) Engel

Hard cover: 978-1-934980-06-4
Soft cover: 978-1-934980-07-1

Library of Congress Control Number: 2016936791

Cover design by Larry@LVMultimedia.com

Printed in the United States of America

Dedicated to Selma and Chaim Engel,

to my parents, Hazel Betty and James Lloyd Markham,

and to my family - past, present, and future.

Of the almost 35,000 or more Dutch Jews taken to Sobibor, and the 250,000 total who perished there, Selma Engel (Saartje Wijnberg) is now (in 2016) the only Dutch-born survivor.

Contents

PREFACE   Eyewitness to Evil. 1

PART ONE   Time Present and Time Past. 5
   Chapter 1   Searching for the Past. 9
   Chapter 2   The Birth of Evil—Hitler's Rise to Power 13

PART TWO   The Darkness Comes 21
   Chapter 3   Memories of My Family. 23
   Chapter 4   New Masters—New Laws 32
   Chapter 5   A Different World 34
   Chapter 6   A Life in Hiding. 38
   Chapter 7   Captured 43
   Chapter 8   Prisoner 45

PART THREE The Hell of Sobibor 49
   Chapter 9   Transport 51
   Chapter 10   Transport Process 55
   Chapter 11   Sobibor 57
   Chapter 12   Sobibor's Dark History. 63
   Chapter 13   Our First Dance. 69
   Chapter 14   Dreams Amid Horrors 72
   Chapter 15   Sobibor Personnel 78
   Chapter 16   Escape Plans. 83
   Chapter 17   The Escape 86
   Chapter 18   Running and Hiding 90

PART FOUR   The Diary. 95

The Loft. 97

Saartje's Diary with Chaim and Saartje's Letters . . . 99

PART FIVE   Different Battles. 135

Liberation 137

Chapter 19   The Liberators 138

Chapter 20   Memories After the War. 147

Chapter 21   The Hardest Journey 153

Chapter 22   Coming Home. 157

Chapter 23   No Longer My Home. 163

Chapter 24   Searching for a Home. 166

Chapter 25   Chaim's Dream. 171

Chapter 26   Speaking Out. 178

Chapter 27   Our Last Dance 186

Chapter 28   Reflections 191

Acknowledgments. 201

Notes   203

Bibliography   207

Sources   211

About the Author 213

Author's Note   215

Eyewitness to Evil

Many will not want to know my story. For some, it is too painful to face the darkness that can exist in the human heart. For others, burying the grief of the past is the only way they can find the strength to build a future. I have heard that many even deny the truth of what I will tell you.

In my life, I have observed and experienced evil so complete that only those with no soul could be responsible. I agree with those who say that we cannot become consumed with the evil of the past but must focus instead on creating a better tomorrow. But in the deepest part of my heart and mind and soul where our personal truths are housed, I know that to ignore or to deny past evil is to open the door and invite that evil into our future.

For those who deny the truth of what I tell you, I can only say that I wish, with every ounce of my being, that this evil had not been born, that the millions who perished because of it could have lived out their normal lives.

Evil denied and un-confronted spreads uncontrollably. It assumes a life of its own and feeds to full strength with every denial and failure to call it by its rightful name. For this reason, my beloved husband Chaim and I spent our lives telling anyone who would listen of our experiences as prisoners at the Nazi Death Camp at Sobibor, Poland, and how we survived. We tell our audiences how love gave us hope, the strength to survive unspeakable horrors, and the courage to dream of surviving to share a normal life. Over and over in our sixty years together, we warned of the dangers of ignoring prejudice and hatred until they grow powerful enough to create the Sobibors, Auschwitzs, Darfurs, and Rwandas of the world.

My Chaim died July 4, 2003, somehow a fitting date because he loved his adopted country so much. America had always been the home of Chaim's dreams for the future, especially during the most brutal and seemingly impossible times. At ninety, I am now too old to travel and speak as much as before, but I must try to speak in some way for the millions who cannot speak for themselves. So, I am telling our story to honor the love that Chaim and I shared and to speak for all those who could not survive the evil.

Selfishly perhaps, I share these memories also because my Chaim is no longer here to protect me from the nightmares, and I am not strong enough to bear them alone. Less selfishly, I have to stand as witness to the horror that is born when hatred is allowed to grow until its power sickens an entire country and becomes its ultimate shame.

Dancing Through Darkness is the true story of a great love, born among the horrors of Sobibor, a Nazi Death Camp, and tested through years of uncertain survival in the war-ravaged Europe of 1943-1944. The story is told in two voices: one is that of ninety-year-old great grandmother Selma Engel (formerly Saartje Wijnberg), who generously shares her memories of the unspeakable suffering and the great joy she has known in her life. The second voice is from Selma's diary, written when she was twenty-one-year-old Saartje Wijnberg, hiding in a hay loft in Poland for nine months while German troops searched for Sobibor escapees. The voices are different due to age and circumstance, but the constant that connects is Chaim Engel, the man whose love gave hope and a dream of survival in a time and place that had destroyed both.

PART ONE

Time Present and Time Past

"The only thing necessary for the triumph of evil
is for good men to do nothing."

EDMUND BURKE,
Letter to William Smith, January 9, 1795

My hand trembles as I turn back the first age-yellowed, crumbling piece of tissue paper… and then another…and another. Lying beneath the layers is a small, fragile-looking book, painfully familiar to me. This book, my diary, had been my constant companion through the most painful and most joyful part of my early life.

Now, it seems too old and too tired to hold so much of my life among its pages… but it does. With my hand resting on the cover and my eyes closed, I am taken back to October, 1943, in Poland. I am again an exhausted, half-starved twenty-one-year-old Dutch girl hiding in a hay loft from the Nazi SS troops who had been ordered to find and shoot all surviving Sobibor Death Camp escapees. My Chaim is sitting next to me on the hay. The air of the small loft is fouled by the smells rising from below and from our own waste bucket. We sit still and quiet, afraid to speak. For ten days after the escape, we hid in the forest by day and ran by night. For now, we are safe.

With this little book, I hold all the suffering, pain, and love of that long-ago time in my hand. Memories from the past overwhelm me as I gently turn back the cover to the first page.

Poland, October 24, 1943

(1)

Suddenly a feeling came over me to write down everything we experienced, my husband and I, in Poland. First of all, I am going to tell you where I am with my dearly beloved husband. We are on a farm, above the horses, in the hay and there is a small hole through which the light enters during the day, just barely enough to see each other. Despite these difficult circumstances we are still thankful and happy that we are alive after having escaped from Sobibor.

CHAPTER 1

Searching for the Past

I had not seen my diary in many years and rarely thought of it. Since Chaim's recent death, I had enough trouble trying to deal with the present. I was afraid the past would defeat me.

One night, several months before my diary was found, the ringing of the phone by my bed, though loud and persistent, seemed part of a dream. By the time I realized the ringing was real, the caller had disconnected, leaving only a blinking message light and a clear, but strange, message.

"I am trying to locate any members of Chaim Engel's family still living in Connecticut. I read of his involvement in the largest and most successful escape from a Nazi Death Camp. I hope to locate his family to learn more about him and his life. If you are related to him or know anyone who has known him, please call me. I want to tell his family how very much I admire his courage." A woman's voice had left a name and phone number.

At this time, three years after Chaim's death, I longed to talk to anybody who would listen to my stories about Chaim and our life together. My friends and family had asked me to talk to a grief counselor because I had not been able to rise above my grief and talk of anything but Chaim. I did as they asked and went weekly to someone who was supposed to help me move forward with my life, as if I could live long enough to forget that Chaim had saved my life... that Chaim *had been* my life.

I dialed the number. "This is Selma Engel. I was married to Chaim Engel for over sixty years. I am now his widow." Soon, Ann Walsh and I were laughing like old friends about our heavy accents—mine Dutch, hers Southern—and the unlikely circumstances that would allow a Jewish woman from Zwolle, Holland, and a Southern woman from Sunflower County, Mississippi, to get in touch and have so much to talk about. We talked about the slim chance of an AP release from Branford, Connecticut, being read in The Atlanta Journal Constitution by someone who cared enough about the life described to search for family and more information. In each of our conversations, I told her that her accent was even harder to understand than mine. She, of course, denied having any accent.

Then I began to talk of Chaim, the kind of man he was, how we met when forced to dance together for the entertainment of the guards at Sobibor Death Camp in Poland, and how we had found a love so strong we could survive anything, even the indescribable deprivation and brutality of Sobibor. I talked and she listened, really listened, to my stories that are so close to my heart.

Being able to talk, with no time limit and no one telling me it was time to build a new life, was pure joy. I knew I had to pull out of my grief. I knew I had to move on with my life. Now, I just needed to be able to talk about Chaim as long as I wanted, to laugh again over our good times and to shed tears over the times that still had the power to haunt me.

After several weeks and many long phone conversations, I invited Ann to visit me in Connecticut. She planned to stay in a hotel, but I laughed at the idea. Just by her interest and compassionate listening, Ann had raised my spirits and made me feel better than I had since Chaim's death. She would stay with me in the home Chaim and I had shared for so many years. "Not open for debate," I told her.

Our first visit was a continuation of the friendship we had started by phone. We talked, visited my friends and family, went out to good restaurants, toured small towns nearby, took my dog Sneakers for walks in my neighborhood, went to nurseries to buy flowers and then drove home to plant them.

One morning as I was telling Ann about my arrival at Sobibor I told her, "I wrote about all this in my diary."

Her eyes widened in astonishment, "What diary?"

"I kept a diary while we were in hiding after the escape and wrote everything that I remembered."

"Oh, Selma, may I see it? Where is it?"

"Of course, you can see it, but I'm not sure where it is. I haven't seen it in years. I do know it's still here somewhere."

"You don't know where it is? Selma, your diary is a piece of history! It belongs in The Holocaust Museum in Washington or Israel, wherever you want, but it deserves being acknowledged for what it meant to you and Chaim and for what it can mean to others."

Shaking my head, I told her, "I'm not so sure about that. The last time I read it, many years ago, it seemed like just a lot of whining and complaining by a spoiled young girl. It's embarrassing to think I was that spoiled young girl."

"I think you are underestimating its importance, Selma. Let's find it; then you can decide what you want to do with it."

I have been in my home since the early 1960s. Finding a small, badly weathered two-by-four inch notebook in the middle of everything Chaim and I had collected over our sixty years together was not going to be easy.

We had perfect weather that day, better for touring beautiful, historic Connecticut towns than searching around in old boxes. The diary could wait. I knew the diary was a part of my history, but I wondered if it could really be important to more than just Chaim and me? Did it belong in a Holocaust Museum, or was it better to leave it where it was, packed away somewhere with other remnants of my past.

The search started after our morning walk and continued until I was tired of searching. Even without having seen it, Ann was convinced that my little book was far more important than I had ever imagined. She said that eyewitness accounts of history are necessary to make history real and to make all of us appreciate those who have gone before. She reminded me of the increase in numbers of Holocaust deniers and revisionists. I wasn't sure where to start looking, but the reasons for finding the little book were strong enough to make the search necessary.

We kept searching.

Right before lunch, our search ended. We found my diary in a box on the floor of a bedroom closet under some winter sweaters. It rested there in its yellowed tissue paper wrapping, looking far from important.

I wanted to translate parts of the diary to show that it was important only to Chaim and me—nothing special and hardly worthy of being in the Holocaust Museum. But, not having read or spoken Dutch in many years, I labored through the now unfamiliar words written on paper almost destroyed by time and hardships. As I struggled to turn the Dutch words into English, I could see Chaim with pencil and paper in his pocket, even after ten days of our running and hiding in the forest. It was all there, not just in my worn little book, but in the deepest part of my memory, in the deepest part of my heart. We stopped when it became too hard to go on. The translating was difficult, but the words, over sixty years after they were written, spoke of too much suffering to be borne easily. We would have to continue later.

As Ann packed to leave the next morning, I sat on the bed in the guest room and told her sincerely, "If you are not able to write our story, or if you write it and no one else is interested, remember that we have each found a special new friend."

The phone calls, the visits, and our unlikely friendship continue. This book, *Dancing Through Darkness*, is the result of two people surviving brutal odds to tell the story of a time when love and hope and dreams survived pure evil; and of another knowing how much the world needs such stories.

CHAPTER 2

The Birth of Evil— Hitler's Rise to Power

As Saartje Wijnberg (Selma Engel) was growing up in the gentle world of Zwolle, Holland, another world, one in which she and her family would soon find themselves trapped and powerless, was being created and marching toward absolute power.

Born May 15, 1922, to proud parents Samuel and Alida Wijnberg and equally proud older brothers, Bram, Maurits, and Marthyn, Saartje was ten and living an idyllic life when Adolf Hitler became Chancellor of Germany. She knew nothing of the events of January 30, 1933, or how they would come to affect her life. The only real change for her was that Saartje, a name she loved, was changed to Selma, a name she did not like, because her paternal grandmother thought it sounded less Jewish. Within thirty days of Hitler's becoming Chancellor, far worse than name changes occurred as the systematic persecution of German Jews began. Jewish businesses were boycotted, and all Jewish personnel were dismissed from local government, law courts, and universities.

Prior to this, the beginning of the Great Depression in 1929 had assured Hitler the support of the desperate German working class. With the membership of the Nazi party almost doubling in that one year, Hitler's plans for assuring Aryan supremacy, first in Germany and then the rest of Europe, moved forward.[1]

The masses believed his lies about restoring Germany to prosperity and power after the devastating results of the Treaty of Versailles, which ended WWI and burdened Germany with deep humiliation and unsustainable reparations. They also believed his lies about Jews being responsible for the economic and political devastation destroying Germany. In Mein Kampf (My Struggle), Hitler calculated his rise to power, including the lies the German people would believe: "The primitive simplicity of their minds renders them a more easy prey to a big lie than a small one, for they themselves often tell little lies but would be ashamed to tell a big one".[2]

By spring of 1933, the Nazi Party majority had voted in the Enabling Act, which gave Hitler the right to legislate on matters of finance, foreign affairs, and the constitution. All political parties, trade unions, and employers' associations were abolished, and the Nazi Party became even more powerful as the old federal constitution was replaced by a system of Nazi laws.

Beginning with those closest to him, Hitler purged all in his party who were in a position to threaten his drive toward absolute power. During the Night of Long Knives on June 30, 1934, seventy Nazis were murdered. Included in this group were many of the original founders of The National Socialist (Nazi) Party. With the aid of his personal bodyguards, the Schutzstaffel (SS), commanded by Heinrich Himmler, those deemed by Hitler and his chief minister, Hermann Goering, to be a threat were systematically identified and brutally murdered. These acts, planned by Himmler and Goering and executed by the SS, set a precedent for the brutal murder of anyone, German or otherwise, who was a perceived threat to Hitler's rise to power.[3]

On August 2, 1934, the office of president was abolished, and all functions were combined under the new position of *Fuehrer*. When the army swore personal allegiance to Hitler as *Fuehrer*, the way was clear for the purge of Germany and the move toward realizing Hitler's territorial ambitions.

From the beginning, Hitler knew the power of public opinion and calculated how to control it. As a master propagandist, he felt the masses needed a few simple ideas represented by powerful symbols. The most powerful symbol of Nazi Germany was the swastika, ever present on the Nazi flag, standards carried in the massive parades, armbands, everywhere. Hitler had designed the Nazi flag with the hooked cross, or *hakenkreuz* at the center, using the ancient symbol to connect Germany's Thousand-Year Reich to the power of the past. The standards were taken from old Roman designs, and the name, the Third Reich, established Nazi Germany as the rightful heir to the First Reich, the Holy Roman Empire; and the Second Reich, established by Otto Von Bismarck in 1871.[4]

The black uniforms, death head insignias, jack boots, and paramilitary ranks were calculated to show the German people the elitism and power of a militaristic society and to strike fear into the hearts of friend and foe alike. Parades were massive demonstrations of power, from the number of troops goose-stepping to German martial music, particularly Wagner, to the pageantry and color of the sea of swastikas used to attract supporters and arouse followers to acts of violence and terror.

Hitler knew the power of words. His designation of undesirables as 'cargo, Jew dog, or rat', and his fiery rhetoric at the massive rallies proclaiming, "We are the children of the gods!" and "You are a member of the Master Race." further dehumanized his archenemy, the Jew, and laid the foundation for the Third Reich. The Hitler Youth pledge, "I belong to Adolf Hitler. I pledge to give up my life…" was meant to secure the future of his self-proclaimed Thousand-Year Reich.

Constant repetition increased the impact of the words and endless "*Seig Heils*" were calculated to create a mob mentality with one mind— Adolf Hitler's.[5]

Saartje was twelve and knew nothing of the brutal power controlling German minds with plans to conquer all of Europe, including her beloved homeland.

With the Nuremberg Laws in 1935, German Jews lost their German citizenship and were forbidden to intermarry with other Germans. They were left with no rights, no contact with non-Jews, and no way to defend themselves against these laws.

Two years later, in 1937, Hitler assured the Netherlands that he would respect their neutrality. They believed his assurances because they had no choice.

On November 9, 1938, during *Kristallnacht* (Night of Broken Glass), over one thousand synagogues and prayer rooms were destroyed in Germany, their libraries burned, seven thousand Jewish businesses trashed and looted, and twenty thousand Jews arrested, all within 48 hours.[6] A young Polish Jew had killed a minor Nazi official, giving the perfect opportunity for the anti-Semitic ideology of the Nazi party to be played out and to instill fear by making examples of all Jews. *Kristallnacht*, as this two day orgy was called because of the broken glass in the streets, created an outcry from some of the German public, but the outcry was neither loud enough nor long enough to slow the rise of Hitler and his Nazi party.[7]

Saartje was now sixteen and heard nothing of this atrocity. News from Germany was totally controlled, and parents protected their children as much as possible from what was happening to the Jews of Germany. Saartje's brothers may have known some of what was happening in Germany, but they would have joined their parents in protecting her.

By the beginning of 1939, German Jews were restricted to living in ghettos and were not allowed in public schools, parks, libraries, museums, hotels, or restaurants. Jews were forbidden to use telephones, radios, or public transportation. All adult Jews were required to register with German authorities, listing business and personal assets. In 1941, all Jewish boys over 12 were conscripted for munitions factory work. The noose around the neck of the German Jewish population had tightened to the point of strangulation.

The people of Zwolle, Saartje's hometown, tried not to think about what was happening in Germany and felt protected by Hitler's repeated promises to respect the neutrality of their country. German Jews had been made prisoners in their own country. Soon the rest of Europe's Jewish population would fall under the same restrictions and worse.

Continuing the march of madness that was sweeping across Europe, Germany prepared a plan in 1938 for the euthanasia of all who were considered incurably ill—all deformed children and all mentally or physically handicapped adults. The code name for the euthanasia program was T-4, so named for its location at Hitler's chancellery at Tiergartenstrasse. Its methods and personnel training were later used in other killing programs and camps.[8]

In spite of Hitler's repeated assurances, German troops invaded the Netherlands on May 10, 1940. The Netherlands surrendered to the Germans five days later on May 15, 1940. It was Saartje's eighteenth birthday.

The Dutch fought bravely; but like the French, Hungarians, Romanians, Czechoslovakians, Belgians, Poles, and others who fell before or after the Dutch invasion, they were neither trained nor equipped to face the juggernaut of the German army or the brutally repressive policies that followed. On May 15, 1940, German troops began the occupation of the Netherlands that was to last until the end of the war.

In *Mein Kampf*, Hitler made it clear that concentration on a single archenemy was necessary to establish and maintain solidarity. Hitler envisioned himself as the common leader and designated the Jews of Europe as the unifying archenemy. "No activity should lead people away from the common struggle against the common enemy, the Jew."[9]

Operation Reinhard, the result of the Wannsee Conference of January 20, 1942, made systematic murder of all Jews German state policy. Over lunch and drinks at a villa in suburban Berlin, fifteen Nazi officials discussed the Final Solution, a euphemism for the systematic extinction of the remaining Jews of Europe. Organizing the conference had been the task of Reinhard Heydrich, but overseeing the execution of the plan fell to Himmler and his SS troops.[10]

Dachau had been built in 1933 and served as a model for SS controlled concentration camps. It was also used as a training ground for all succeeding camp personnel and guards. Achieving maximum efficiency for degrading, murdering, and disposing of the bodies of the Jewish population was crucial if the Final Solution was to become a reality. By the spring of 1940, Auschwitz was completed. On June 14, the trains began arriving at Auschwitz with freight cars and cattle cars carrying thousands of men, women, and children to their deaths.

By the end of 1944, there were tens of thousands of labor, concentration, and death camps and sub-camps throughout the Nazi-controlled lands. All camps existed to use the prisoners as slave labor or to degrade and slaughter Jews and other undesirables, but the four Death Camps—Sobibor, Treblinka, Chelmno, and Belzec—existed solely for the immediate and increasingly efficient extermination of as many prisoners as possible.

Only the few needed to take care of the camp, see to the needs of the guards, operate the gas chambers, haul the bodies of their fellow Jews to the fires, and sort the valuables of those slaughtered were kept alive at these four camps.

With the arrival of each transport at the death camps, SS guards sorted prisoners and pulled those with needed skills and those who looked healthy enough to work out of line. The rest, including pregnant women, women with children, the sick, and the elderly, went directly to the gas chambers. When the small window in the door of the gas chamber showed no remaining movement, the prisoners saved to do the work of the camp threw the bodies on trolleys and hauled them to common graves or to the fires that burned constantly.[11] Burying the bodies in common graves and covering them with lime had been deemed too slow for the numbers being slaughtered in the death camps.

The fires also left less evidence of the Final Solution than common graves.[12]

Racism and German supremacy, the major themes of Nazi ideology, dictated the conduct of the war, motivated German policy in occupied countries, and ultimately resulted in the Holocaust. Hitler had used anti-Semitism, one of the cornerstones of Nazi ideology, in entering every European country. The goal was not just degradation, but total annihilation of all Jews. Also included in the plans for annihilation were those not in line with the German Aryan ideal or who committed the heresy of opposing the Nazi regime in any way. In spite of the courageous resistance of many, civilization seemed to falter as some members of the human race descended into the darkness of barbarism on a scale unknown in recorded history.

Hitler's view of History's judgment was far from the truth: "The judges of this state may go right ahead and convict us of our actions at that time, but History, acting as the goddess of a higher truth and a higher justice, will one day smilingly tear up this verdict, acquitting us all of guilt and blame."[13]

In 1942, the brutality of this world consumed the peaceful world of Saartje Wijnberg and her family when Nazi SS troops abruptly entered the family's hotel in Zwolle, Holland. They ordered the Wijnbergs to be out of their home in one hour, taking only what each of them could carry.

PART TWO

The Darkness Comes

"Speak up for those who cannot speak for themselves, for the rights of all who are destitute."

PROVERBS 31:8

CHAPTER 3

Memories of My Family

In Zwolle, Holland, a town that I knew and loved, my parents, Samuel and Alida Wijnberg, owned a small Kosher hotel. We were proud of the gentle beauty of our town with its flower-filled parks and important-looking old buildings, many dating back to the fourteenth and fifteenth centuries. Later to become the capital of the province of Overijssel, Zwolle had been granted city rights in 1230 and the original town hall was completed in 1448. Due to its location on a hill bordered by three rivers, it became an important trade center with a cattle market second in size only to the one in Rotterdam.

The cattle market was important to the success of Hotel Wijnberg, and my parents worked long hours as the buyers and sellers used the hotel as a base for meetings and meals. From an early age, I took pride in the beauty and history of our town and knew the importance of the cattle market to our family business.

My friends and I loved Zwolle, and we spent as much time as our parents allowed on the hiking and biking trails and at the beaches. Until my eighteenth birthday, this was my world. Even now I smile when I think of our address, Veermarktstraat 23, and how our hotel looked. Our phone, number 4101, rang as often as you would expect with a successful hotel and a busy family of six.

My mother, loving and family centered, ran our family and most areas of the hotel with a strong but gentle hand. My father, in charge of the kitchen and banquets, contributed his knowledge and organization, but with an unnecessary harshness that we avoided when possible. As different as my parents were, their combined talents and hard work created a close family and steady success for Hotel Wijnberg.

In 1933, my name was changed for reasons that I did not understand fully at the time. One day I was simply told that I would now answer to Selma. I never liked Selma and always loved Saartje, so I am now Saartje again, at least part of the time. I still think it's funny that the name they gave me to sound less Jewish was one of the most common female Jewish names in America when Chaim and I arrived many years later. The difference was that in our new home, we did not have to hide being Jewish or fear being arrested.

My arrival in the Wijnberg family had been preceded by three boys, Bram, Maurits, and Marthyn, who were nine, seven, and five respectively at the time of my birth. Abraham or Bram, as I called him, was the oldest and always tender and patient with me. During my early years, he was more like a father figure than a brother. Our father was a cold, distant man, never showing approval or outward signs of love, so Bram filled the vacancy by being especially loving to and protective of his little sister.

As I got older, I thought he sometimes carried the protective part too far, particularly when I got old enough to be interested in boys. He definitely carried it too far when boys became interested in me and he played the role of my stern protector.

Bram was handsome as a boy, and became even more so as a man. He always seemed so sophisticated to me and my friends. As we got older, they all drove him crazy with their giggles and attempts to gain his attention. They were even envious when Bram chose me to help him teach dance lessons at our hotel. He could have had any number of girls help him, but he insisted that I was the only partner he wanted. Part of the reason for his choice was that I needed to learn to dance. As a confirmed tomboy, I saw no need and never wanted to take the time to bother with it. The other part of the reason was that he just liked to tease me. My friends may have been envious as I whirled around the dance floor with the handsome Abraham Wijnberg, but I was far more envious as they biked to the beach for the afternoon. I had to get dressed up and keep smiling until the dance lessons were over. My so-called friends used the same time for nothing more serious than sunning and laughing.

Bram broke many young hearts, especially among my friends, when he married Jettie Vries in a big, beautiful wedding in Amsterdam on May 8, 1940. Now he had a wife who was first in his life. While I was joyful that our family was growing, I did have to admit, but only to myself, that I might be a little jealous. I don't think I was really jealous, but I missed having my big brother all to myself sometimes.

Maurits, my middle brother, was always the most gentle with our mother. He treated her the same way she treated all of us, with great love and tenderness. We all loved and respected her, but he was especially sweet and thoughtful. He may have been making up for some of our father's harshness, or maybe it was just that our mother deserved gentleness and kindness.

Maurits had been in love with a girl named Bep Jacobs since they were sixteen. In spite of the rules imposed on Jews, and with the situation growing worse every day, they decided in 1941 to get married anyway. The laws imposed by the Germans prevented Maurits and Bep's living together after their marriage, but we still thought the laws would be abolished or at least relaxed in time.

We loved Bep and her family and were happy for the marriage, but we were afraid that the good times for all of us were going to be delayed for a while. We made their wedding as happy as it could be under the circumstances, but Bep had to continue living with her family and Maurits with his. In spite of the danger of breaking curfew, many nights Maurits would leave well after dark, staying off the most carefully patrolled streets, to see Bep at her parents' home. Anyone on the street after 5 pm was subject to being arrested and deported, or shot immediately. My mother walked the floor every night until he got home. She never asked him not to go, but she begged him to be careful.

At night, we could hear the sharp clicking of German boots as they patrolled the streets and the loud crack as their heels snapped together for stops or turns. We hated the sound of those boots, the sound of being under the heel of a merciless enemy. We all lived in fear of the silence when the boots stopped. We knew if Maurits was caught trying to get to or from Bep's home, that silence of the boots and the knock that came with it would be at our door to destroy us all.

My youngest brother, Marthyn, only five years older than I, was the most talented of the family. He played piano and saxophone, loved to cook, and went to culinary school to become a pastry chef. I never told anyone what I thought, but he was even more handsome and charming than his older brothers. The girls were crazy about him, but he wasn't serious about anybody, so I had this handsome big brother all to myself on many long, early morning bike rides. Those clear, cool mornings with both of us riding hard and laughing harder were as close to perfect as the rest of my world was then.

Hotel Wijnberg was always full of people in town for the local cattle market or people attending meetings, dinners, and parties. Because our hotel was the only Kosher hotel in the area, we had a steady stream of customers, families, friends, and salesmen. There was rarely a time alone for any of us, but we liked it that way. When there were large dinners or special functions, my brothers and I helped any way we could, following either my mother's or my father's directions. I didn't always like what I was asked to do, especially if it meant working with my father, who was impossible to please, or missing time with my friends during the dance lessons. I adored Bram, but at sixteen and seventeen, there were too many other things I wanted to do with my friends.

I remember the time I tried to get out of the dance lessons forever by telling my mother all the reasons someone else, someone who loved dancing, would be a better partner for Bram. My mother didn't force me. She just listened patiently and then told me the choice was mine. She followed that by telling me how much it helped Bram and the hotel and our family. My mother would have done anything for us. How could I not do as she asked? So I continued to act as my brother Bram's dance partner and tried not to complain about it. Bram teased me about what a good dancer I was becoming. He promised that someday I would learn to love dancing and be grateful to him for all he had taught me. I did not know then that a single dance would someday change my life forever.

With three older brothers, I stayed a tomboy long after my mother felt I should have become interested in becoming a young lady. I was not remotely interested in being a young lady and was often teased by my brothers and their friends about the devilish sparkle in my eyes. Some say that sparkle is still there; I hope it survived. Too much of that world did not.

In 1941, my father passed away suddenly, leaving my mother to manage the hotel and our family alone. My father had been a decent young man, I think, or maybe I just hope that he had been; but as he had grown older, he had developed an eye for the ladies. In addition to humiliating my mother, who deserved none of this, he had become increasingly stern and hard with Bram, Maurits, Marthyn, and even me. I remember my mother's gentleness always being present to take the edge from my father's harshness. She would also try, unsuccessfully, to protect her children from the brutality of Hitler's world as it consumed ours. As her only daughter and the youngest of four, I was treated with even more tenderness than my older brothers. She was proud of her sons, but I think I was her special joy. She loved me with pride, fierce protectiveness, and occasional dismay over my free spirit and laughing, tomboy ways. Alida Nathan Wijnberg held our lives, our business, and our family together.

How I would have loved introducing my mother to my beloved Chaim and hearing her pronounce him a "good man." When my children were small, I dreamed of watching her hold and love my babies. She would have been as good an Oma as she was a mother. I have always tried to be a really good Oma because I felt I was filling the role for myself and for my mother, who never had the chance to hold or to know her grandchildren. My early memories of my family are as close to my heart now as they were then. I think often of my smart, handsome, funny older brothers. I think of all the good people we knew who passed through our hotel. I think of the gentleness and strength of my mother. And I think of all who did not survive.

Saartje Wijnberg as a young girl in Zwolle, Holland
1934

Saartje with her three older brothers.
Bram, Maurits and Marthyn

Before the German Invasion
with friends at the beach
Saartje is third from the right

Biking with friends
Saartje is second from the right

CHAPTER 4

New Masters—New Laws

With the May, 1940, German invasion of my homeland came new laws that had been tried and perfected on the German population and then on other annexed or conquered countries. The Nuremberg Laws applied particularly to the Jewish populations that Hitler had designated as the arch-enemy and had been used successfully to unify widely diverse nationalities and groups. The Dutch Jews of the Netherlands were now included in Hitler's Master Plan to create a Judenfrei Europe. I remember the changes clearly. Even now, over 65 years later, I can count them off on my fingers.

First, all Dutch Jews over six now wore the yellow Star of David. Anyone caught on the streets without it was arrested. We had to sew the Star of David on our clothes so we could not remove it easily. Second, anyone caught on the streets after curfew was arrested and deported, or shot. We still had no idea what deported or relocated meant, but we would learn soon enough. Number three was designed to destroy any way for Jews to get news or to travel around town, so all radios and bicycles were taken from us. Number four restricted our access to stores. The few stores that were open to Jews had almost nothing, and the small amount available was of terribly inferior quality. Number five took our books away because Jews were no longer allowed in public libraries, and many of our books had been burned. Number six kept us from entering our own museums, and number seven denied entry to any hotels or restaurants. I had grown up in a hotel owned by my family and now I was forbidden to enter one!

Public schools were forbidden for Jewish children, and we could not associate with non-Jews, so numbers eight and nine meant being shut off from our school and many of our good friends. Number ten took our beautiful parks away from us. We were no longer allowed in them.

Too many new laws to count on both hands. Number eleven: we couldn't get jobs because we were forbidden work permits; and even if we could have gotten work permits, number twelve did not allow us to enter government buildings, so there was no way we could pick up a work permit. Number thirteen: We couldn't travel because we were not allowed to get travel permits, but we had no way to travel even if the permits had not been banned for Jews. The last one on my list for now is that anything owned by a Jew had to be registered with our new masters. The Germans were free to take anything they wanted; having everything registered just made it easier for them to determine items of value.

Now we, like the countries conquered before us, were prisoners in our own country and being dehumanized as quickly as possible. We had no rights and no laws to protect us since Hitler had changed our laws; we could only hope for a quick end to this insanity.

I questioned over and over, "How can they do this to us? How can they?" This was our home. We had grown up playing in Zwolle's parks, using the libraries, going to the museums, strolling the streets with friends and family. We had done nothing to deserve these new laws. I knew every Dutch Jew was asking the same question, but we all knew there was no answer. We were a law-abiding people, so we tried to obey the new laws. But we had also learned to fear these stern, hard invaders of our country and to hate their air of superiority and their cruel inhuman laws.

CHAPTER 5

A Different World

The change that altered our lives forever came early in 1942, when, with no warning, a German officer came to our hotel and told us they needed it to house troops. Since Jews could no longer own property, an exclusive men's club had already taken over the hotel, but we had been allowed to remain in our living quarters. Now we were told we had one hour to be out, and we were to take only what we could carry. We were told nothing else.

I remember my mother trying to decide what would be most important. Were family pictures important enough to replace things we might need more? Should we try to carry food, or hope we would be able to buy enough? Food supplies were limited now, so we never knew what would be available. Bare necessities took precedence over everything. What did we absolutely have to have for survival until this was over? What clothes, blankets, coats were necessary? How much could each of us carry? Where could we go? These were impossible decisions, but they had to be made, and quickly, or the German soldiers would make them for us.

In a panic, I rushed from one room to another, gathering up those things we had decided to take with us. We took a few family pictures, but most of the heavy loads each of us carried held what we thought was necessary for our survival. We wore all the clothes we could get on and then packed extra pairs of socks and good boots, warm blankets, and two large pots for cooking.

I refused to cry because I knew it would make a terrible situation even worse for my mother. In the middle of making these life and death decisions, she was trying to be brave and calmly help us do what had to be done.

The Germans were determined to destroy everything of value to us. They wanted to leave us with no self respect, no pride, and no humanity. Now, my mother, like all parents under German rule, had lost even the right to protect her children.

I choked on my rage and fear and helplessness. I don't know how to describe the feeling. There was nowhere to turn, no one who could help us. We were trapped, with no choice but to do as ordered. We knew we had no power and could do nothing to protect what was dearest to us: the people we loved, our home, and our country. We were prisoners in a war we didn't understand. No one could imagine the eventual consequences of being caught in this war, the war we had lost the minute Hitler had started his climb to absolute power. We were not told how long we would be gone, or where we could go to live in a town that had no places left for dispossessed Jews.

With half our allotted time gone, we were still trying to make decisions. Time was running out. Should we put on even more clothes? Were there important papers we were forgetting? Should we use our suitcases for carrying food and valuables? Would paper money be worth anything?

Our mother told us to stay calm and think, that panic would be our worst enemy. She said we could face anything as long as we used our heads and stayed together, but she did not know this new enemy or the world it had created. We were to learn that no enemy was as powerful as the one that now controlled us. Whether we panicked or used our heads or tried to stay together, none of it mattered anymore.

I was frightened for myself and my family, but I was also angry, fiercely angry. For the first of many times, my fear smothered the anger. With hard-eyed smiles covering their cruelty, the officers and the soldiers took over our hotel as casually as if we were going on holiday, and they had been invited to care for it in our absence. I hated these black-booted, steely-eyed robots with a cold, hard vengeance. I prayed for the power to destroy everyone who was a part of this cruelty. But absolute power was in their hands.

We had no idea what was happening, or we would not have agonized so over what we had to leave behind. We did know enough to obey immediately, and without question, what we were ordered to do by the Germans. Their reputation and their manner left no room for anything other than immediate and total obedience. My fear smothered the anger and the hatred and took control. At the end of the hour we had been given, we walked away from our home of a lifetime with only what we could carry. We still naively and foolishly thought they would let us come back when they no longer needed our hotel for the soldiers.

Many families in Zwolle, our friends and neighbors, were also being displaced from their homes to give the German troops the best places to stay. A place to move into, any place, was almost impossible to find. We were hoping to find something that would be large enough for all of us. We still thought we would be able to survive the cruelty and the insanity if we could stay together.

Finally, after asking everyone we knew, we found a small shack. It had no hot water and no bathroom. Dark and damp, it was not big enough for all of us, but it was all that was available. We were among the luckier ones. Some were still trying to find a place when 5 pm curfew came, and they had to get off the streets any way they could. People who came to our door just before curfew time were never turned away.

Compared to what we had been used to at our hotel, this place was terrible. It overflowed with four adults and our few belongings crammed in it. From large spaces and separate bedrooms, we were now tripping over each other and the bags we had carried with us from the hotel. As uncomfortable as it was, we knew we were lucky to have found anything and began to make the adjustments needed to live a life with no comforts, no news of what was happening, and in constant fear of the Germans, who owned us and our country now.

We were a close and loving family, but the small space and the restrictions imposed by curfew, limited food, and no bikes or radios began to wear on everybody. We did everything we could to keep our spirits up—straightening our belongings, mending clothes, playing games, telling stories—but uncertainty about our future hung like a dark, heavy cloud over every waking minute. We were desperate for news, but all we heard were rumors of people being sent to labor camps to help the German war effort.

In my mind, I again asked questions, "If they can impose these harsh new laws, if they can take our home and order us to be out in one hour, if they can treat us as if we are less than human with no feelings and no rights, is there any limit to what their cruelty can do to us?" I was afraid I knew the answer.

CHAPTER 6

A Life In Hiding

We all tried to find work, but without work permits, there was little to find. I was finally able to find a place helping an older couple in Apeldoorn that didn't require a permit. I was to live with them and do all the cooking, cleaning, and laundry. If I remember correctly, their name was Lezer.

This was the first time I had lived away from my family, and my rare visits home were not enough to ease the deep loneliness that was a part of my every waking moment. Some things about those times are as clear in my memory as my oatmeal this morning; others swirl through foggy confusion and stubbornly resist being brought to the surface. In the past I have not wanted to deal with the painful memories of that time and place. They were easier to bear when buried. Now I must try to raise these memories, no matter how difficult they are to retrieve and bear. I owe my memories to all who did not survive this time. My memory must be a complete and honest witness to what happened and what was done to us.

I was used to working at the hotel and was a good, thorough Dutch cleaner, but I had never been treated like a servant before. I tried hard to please the old couple, but nothing I did mattered. They ignored me except when gruff orders were being given. I never received a thank you or a kind word or an acknowledging look. Orders were given for what had to be done and then other orders added until there was no possible way to get everything done; then came the reprimands and the scoldings. I had become accustomed to harsh, unfeeling treatment from the German soldiers, but I was disappointed to find such treatment from my own people. I accepted the loneliness and the lack of kindness because it helped my family.

Going to our tiny, crowded shack on the rare occasions I could get away safely was all I had to look forward to. During the bleak and endless days of cleaning, cooking, washing, ironing, and trying futilely to please the Lezers, I wondered what was going to happen to me and my family. Knowing nothing of our fate and being powerless to control anything became my way of life, but I never got used to it.

My rare trips home were worth any sacrifice. For a few hours, I was again a well-loved daughter and little sister, surrounded by my mother and brothers. We drew strength from being together. In spite of little food and no comforts, being able to share the love and closeness of my family gave me the strength I needed to help any way I could.

By early afternoon on the day I visited my family, I began watching the clock to be sure I didn't get caught out after curfew. I waited as late as I could to leave until my mother, with a sad voice and encouraging words, would tell me it was time. My tears stayed near the surface, but I couldn't add to my family's hard time, especially my mother's, by allowing them to spill over. We clung to each other as long as we could, and then I walked out the door. I never told my mother about the situation at the Lezers, or she would have asked me to come back and find something else. She was a gentle woman, but the harsh treatment of her daughter by some of our own people would have smothered her gentleness with disbelief and then anger.

One day outside the Lezers' house in Apeldoorn, a Catholic priest came up to me and told me he was concerned and thought I should go into hiding. He knew nothing else, but he had heard rumors of forced deportations and labor camps. He thought I would be safer with a non-Jewish family and offered to find a family willing to take me in until things got better.

There was no way to reach my mother or brothers to ask their advice, so I accepted because I thought anything would be an improvement over the current situation. I had come to resent the old couple who demanded so much and gave nothing in return. That afternoon, the priest came to me and told me he had found someone from Zwolle who was willing to hide me. The priest must have had a list of people willing to help, because that same day he came to take me on his bike to the young woman's apartment in Utrecht, where she now lived. The apartment was small but light and pleasant. I, once again, had my own room and enough food. There was even a radio, but with only German-controlled stations.

The young woman, who was a nurse and at work much of the time, treated me like a guest in her home, like a friend—no orders, no being ignored. I remember her kindness being like a piece of home after my stay with the Lezers. Her name was Miss Degroot, and we even invented a story about why I was staying with her if we were discovered. We decided I was the daughter of her parents' friends. My mother was sick, and I would be staying with her until my mother was better. But even with our story, I was to remain inside when she was not there. I tried to show Miss Degroot how much I appreciated her help by keeping the apartment spotlessly clean, doing laundry, and by looking for any thing I could do to repay her courage and her kindness. As hard as I worked, I knew there was no way I would ever be able to repay this kind of debt.

Many people ignored the hardships of the Jews. Some even turned their backs on former Jewish friends, but people who wanted to help found ways. Good, right-thinking people were aware of the madness spreading throughout Europe. Confronting the madness directly was a death wish, so these people did as much as they could, silently and secretly. The thousands who risked their lives to help Jews hide or escape didn't do it expecting to be repaid. They did it because their hearts and minds and souls told them they had to do something, anything to help combat this evil.

Miss Degroot shared with me what she heard at work, the whispers that Jews were being rounded up and taken to labor camps. There were whispers, but we knew nothing. Being unsure of anything created an underlying fear constantly fueled by unanswered questions. In spite of Miss Degroot's kindness, the one dream of my heart was still to get back to Zwolle and my mother and brothers. I had no way to contact them and no way to find out what was happening to them. Had they been allowed to stay in our tiny shack, or had they also been forced to go into hiding?

Did they know where I was? Were they searching for me?

Alone most days while Miss Degroot was at work, I was tormented by unanswerable questions. Cleaning and looking for ways to help around the apartment created the only controllable order in my life. Maybe, I thought, if I cleaned hard enough, I could get down to the unspeakable filth of the Germans who were causing all this. With the Germans cleaned out, we could all get back to our wonderfully normal lives. Not being able to get outside for even short walks, when my life had been lived on the hiking and biking trails and the beaches of Zwolle, made even the pleasant apartment seem like a prison, or so I thought at the time.

Late one night after she got home from the hospital, Miss Degroot called me into the kitchen for a cup of tea. As we faced each other across her small table, she told me of a Jewish friend with a husband and two small children who had asked her to hide them. She could not refuse her friend, and there was not enough room in the apartment to hide five people without being discovered and reported.

I was saddened that any of us, especially children, had to be in hiding because of what we were born to be, but I understood why I was the one who had to leave. I had felt safe in this place, and Miss Degroot and I had enjoyed our time together in spite of the circumstances. Now, her friend, with her husband and two children, had to move in as quickly as another hiding place could be found for me.

I knew there were things happening that I did not understand, but I did not realize at the time that anyone who sheltered a Jew risked his life and that of his entire family if discovered. The courage of the people who dared to help in spite of the price, if caught, still overwhelms me. Even now I ask myself if I would have had the courage to risk everything for strangers. So many did. I hope my courage would have been enough to make me one of them.[14]

Miss Degroot took me to an older couple in Bilthoven that she knew from her work. I think if she had known them well, she would have tried to find someone kinder to hide me. In Bilthoven, I had a repeat of the situation with the Lezers. I had to clean a huge, very old, very dirty house.

I was allowed no outside contact and almost no food. The house was always cold, and again I was treated as a servant. I was so unhappy, more alone than ever, and once again completely ignored except when orders were given. Knowing no one, getting no news about what was happening, and often with nothing to eat but an apple or a soup made of old bones, I was beginning to know how real hunger felt. For a while I tried to hide a little bread under my pillow so I wouldn't go to sleep hungry and wake up from stomach pains. When my hidden bread started to attract some of the rats from the basement, I decided it was easier to handle my hunger pains.

Nothing made any sense anymore. A few short months ago, my life had been full of only good things, a warm and loving family and the freedom to do whatever I wanted as long my mother approved. Now, not yet 20, I was in hiding and being treated like a criminal, but I had committed no crime.

My greatest sadness came when a man from Zwolle somehow found me and told me that my mother and brothers had been taken to Poland. I did not know why they had been taken, or where I could go to find them. Hope deserted me and I felt truly alone for the first time in my life.

We can't survive long without hope, so I created false hope. I spent my time imagining how it would be when my family was all back together, laughing and living our old life. I imagined dancing with Bram for the lessons and trying to hold in the laughter with my brothers when our father issued orders and then marched self-importantly from the room. I imagined riding my bike as fast as I could and laughing with the wind in my face, challenging my friends to catch me. My family and friends had been my world. Now, I had neither.

What was to become of me? What had happened to my family, my beloved mother and brothers and the wives of Bram and Maurits? Would I ever see my mother and brothers again? Where were the girls I had grown up with, played with, told secrets to, and laughed with? Would I ever have another chance to go the beach or bike with my friends? How long could I survive on false hope?

CHAPTER 7

Captured

My days followed the same routine of taking orders and resenting the heartlessness of the old couple. I was never allowed outside until the day they told me that I could go next door to visit some people hiding there. I had learned not to ask, but I wondered, *Why next door? What people?* I had not seen another person since I had moved into their home. *Why today?*

In spite of the questions, I was excited about finally getting out of the old house for even a few minutes and having a chance to see some new faces. I waited impatiently for the time to go next door. Maybe the people were from Zwolle and had news of my family. Maybe they were even people I had known in my other life.

The instant I walked in their neighbor's door, the excitement left me. Members of the NSB, one of the worst groups in our country for helping the Germans, entered just behind me. These were my own countrymen, members of the Dutch police, who had arrested me. I learned later that the man next door to the old house where I had been staying had turned in 28 Jews and been paid for each one. I was the 29th. For me and four others who were arrested at the same time, he received the equivalent of about sixty dollars. Still very young and trusting, I thought naively that he was the only one guilty of selling Jews and wondered what the old couple thought when I did not return. The policemen questioned each of us. Where were we from? What were the names of the people who had been hiding us? Where were our families? Although physically sickened by fear, I knew what I had to do. So nervous I could hardly speak, I told the officers questioning me that I didn't know any names.

I would never have repaid the kindness of the nurse from Zwolle who had hidden me in her apartment in Utrecht by giving the police her name. I was not sure if the old couple had knowingly sent me next door as a part of their neighbor's plan to help the Nazis round up Jews. I knew they were capable of unfeeling harshness, but I hoped they were not capable of selling a fellow human being. So I gave no names and was learning for the first time in my life that many of my own people could not be trusted.

Even now, I am a little surprised and proud that I had the courage to lie to these Dutch policemen. Fear was almost smothering me, but I tried to steady my voice and act as if I had nothing to fear. I still thought, again naively, that the Underground's taking the J for Jude off my papers would keep me safe. After I convinced the arresting officers that I really knew no names, they asked for my identification papers. When the papers were held up to the light, he could see where the J had been removed. I was arrested.

Me! Saartje Wijnberg of Zwolle, Holland, beloved daughter of Alida and Samuel Wijnberg, younger sister of Bram, and Maurits, and Marthyn Wijnberg, had been arrested and was being taken to jail! I had felt vulnerable before, but it was nothing like this. I was in the custody of people representing the Germans, conquerors of my country, creators of cruel new laws, destroyers of our families and homes. I was more powerless than ever. Afraid to move until shoved toward the door, I moved as if in a trance.

This could not be real; I had done nothing wrong. In the world I knew, only common criminals were arrested, and they had a chance to prove their innocence in court. This was not the world I knew. And there was no doubt about my crime. I was a Jew.

CHAPTER 8

Prisoner

The Underground contacted me through one of the guards at the jail in Utrecht. The guard was excited as he told me that the Underground could help me escape and get out of the country. Not yet twenty, desperately alone and frozen by hopelessness and confusion, my only thought was to find where my mother and brothers had been taken and join them. I refused the offer of escape.

After all that had happened—the hiding, the arrest, the fear, the hunger—I still tried to convince myself that the bad times would soon be over. I thought that when this insanity passed, we would be allowed to return to our hotel and the life we had known. I would not have survived if I had known what was really happening, or what the next few years would bring.

The Dutch police were all business, arrogant and harsh, but not cruel. It was as if they were just doing a job, and their job now was to find and arrest Jews. Some of the guards at the jail were sympathetic, others harsh. They shuttled us from cell to cell and then from jail to jail. We were never told where we were going or why we were being moved.

I was taken from Bilthoven to Utrecht and then to a jail in Amsterdam, where I stayed for the next three or four months. As I look back, those days in an Amsterdam jail were the best times I had had since my arrest and the best I would have for a long, dark time. I walked into the cell, quietly searching for a friendly face. There were eight girls in the cell, all staring at me, the newcomer. We didn't know each other but, somehow, the nine of us in this particular cell clicked. I felt safer in this cell than anywhere I had been since being arrested. We had little food and were always hungry. Luckily, a woman who worked at the jail had known Bram, my oldest brother, at hotel school. She smuggled badly needed food to us when she could. We shared the food equally, so each of us could have a small bit to ease the hunger.

The nine of us shared our stories and felt better just not being alone. We were a mixed group, from different cities and towns and backgrounds. None had led a life as protected as mine, and the mix included a couple of what we called public women. They shared their stories along with the rest of us, and we were alternately fascinated and shocked by what we heard. The younger and more innocent of us tried to act as if their stories were nothing new to us, that we were not as fascinated by their experiences as we really were. I don't think we fooled them, as they continued to share their stories of some of the seamier sides of life in the Netherlands.

The most mature woman in the cell was a doctor's wife, lovely but sad. She had two young children and didn't know where they or her husband were. None of us knew where our families were, but we were sad for her because of her children. Another woman was so beautiful and so sophisticated that we stood in awe of her and her stories of life in Amsterdam as part of an important and very wealthy family. She convinced us to start doing daily exercises to help keep us strong. Anything that could help us stay a little healthier and more positive was important for our survival.

The cell was small and crowded. With nine people, we had little room to move, but we did manage to follow her lead and do a little bit of bending and stretching and toe touching. I think that even that little bit helped keep us healthier and more positive. At least, it brought some order to our lives and gave us something to do for a little while every day.

The Dutch people love being outside. I had been such an outdoor person that the confinement of the jails threatened my stability. My time in hiding had been bad, but this was far worse. As simple as the exercises were, they helped release some of the pent-up energy that before had been used for the hiking, biking, swimming, and working in our hotel.

I was the country girl, gently teased about the knee socks knitted by my mother. I shared my story, listened to all theirs, and realized that all girls were not from homes that had protected them from the harder sides of life as mine had. In this jail cell, I was quickly learning more about the ways of the world than my mother and father had ever wanted me to know. Regardless of how different the backgrounds and stories were, at least none of us had to face the terrors of the unknown alone.

Christmas was a good time for us; we had better food than usual to celebrate the Christian holiday, and I became friends with Ulla. She was only sixteen at the time, and I felt like a protective big sister. We smoked and told stories, wondering about these Germans who now controlled our lives. We tried to figure out what was happening to our world and what was going to happen to us. We bravely told each other if the stories of Jews being sent to work camps were true, then we Dutch, who were not afraid of hard work, had nothing to fear. We thought if we worked hard, we would be safe until this was all over.

I think now that we must have been wrapped in a cocoon of ignorance created by denial and the optimism of youth. To defend our ignorance, if it needs any defense, we had no news of the outside. Like many who heard the rumors and ignored them, we would not have been able to accept the truth even if we had heard it. I think maybe we were given only what we could bear.

From the jail in Amsterdam, we were all taken to Furcht, a camp near the Belgian border. One of the men at this camp had come to our hotel as a salesman, remembered me, and asked if I wanted to be head of the laundry. He knew the Underground could get me out fairly easily if I worked in the laundry, and he looked the other way. So I was made head of the laundry and again was given a chance to escape.

With no money, even less courage and feeling completely alone except for the girls from the jail, I clung desperately to my dream of finding my mother and brothers and foolishly turned down what was to be my last chance to escape. I thought if I escaped, I would be alone again. I couldn't face that; at least here I had friends. Even with my new friends around me,

I began to have a terrible sense of the darkness facing us. I felt our descent was now in a downward spiral, going deeper and deeper into a darkness that would engulf us totally. I felt trapped and could think of no way out that I was brave enough to try alone.

By this time, I, the girl who could not believe she had been arrested, had been in different jails for a total of over seven months.

PART THREE

The Hell of Sobibor

"The one means that wins the easiest victory over reason: terror and force."

ADOLF HITLER,
Mein Kamph, 1933

CHAPTER 9

Transport

After one week at Furcht, having turned down my last chance for escape, I, along with all the girls from the jail, was put in a freight car and taken by train to Westerbork, a transit camp in Holland. All of us who had been in the Amsterdam jail together tried to stay together. When we noticed two girls from another cell moving under their blanket, we wondered what they were doing. One of our two public women explained to us that they were homosexuals. Our innocence seems strange now, but at nineteen I still didn't know what that meant.

All Dutch Jews who were to be deported went to Westerbork first. This camp was larger than the one at Furcht with cots and a bathroom but no time for showers. Our time was spent in long lines as we gave our names and endless information about ourselves, our homes, and our families. The Germans and the people who worked for them were great record keepers when they wanted to be.

We were at Westerbork only a few days before our deportation orders came. Sixty of us were ordered to the loading platform. We were all herded into one freight car with nothing but straw on the floor and a low barrel in the corner for a toilet. There was little room to sit or lie down so we stood, pressed together too tightly to fall. Small children had to be held by parents to be able to breath and to avoid being crushed by larger bodies.

Shortly after being loaded, I saw my mother's brother with his wife and four children near the center of the crowd. I finally caught his attention and waved. This was the first family I had seen in months, and my initial excitement over being with my aunt and uncle and their children almost made me forget the crowding and the smell of the train. My excitement died as I looked at their faces. How could they, already so thin and lifeless, survive with no food or water or good air? I was almost glad to be alone except for the girls from the jail in Amsterdam. We took turns trying to get out of cramped positions, but the fear and the hunger silenced most of the talking. What was there to say?

We left Westerbork on April 3, 1943, and for three days and three nights, we had nothing to eat and no room to move. I was in such a state of shock that I don't remember everything. I am not sure whether we had water, but I do remember there was no food. The hunger was worse than any I had known up to that time. The sounds of parents trying to comfort crying children were not as bad as the babies who no longer had the strength to cry and died quietly in their mother's arms. The smells of death and sickness fed our fears and became almost unbearable as we moved toward wherever the Germans had decided we were to be, a place we did not know.

The clicking of the wheels on the track had always lulled me to sleep on the rare train rides I enjoyed before the war; now the same sounds seemed to be an ominous warning of what was to come. At every stop, someone would look out the one small, high window and describe the scene for the rest of us. It was always the same, regardless of where the train stopped. The person looking out would speak in a low voice of seeing people, some with their hands on their heads, milling about in confusion until they were forced into lines. German guards were everywhere with guns, and whips, and big dogs. We couldn't see, but what we heard was as terrifying as the scene that was being described. Over the noise of the train, we heard as women screamed for their husbands and children, children cried from fear and hunger, and the commanding voices of the German soldiers barked orders as their snarling dogs forced people into lines. Occasionally, we heard a shot.

No matter how hard we tried, we could not shut out the sounds, the descriptions of the sights, or the thoughts of what was ahead. It was torture being on the freight car, not knowing where we were going, or why.

It was even worse to think about what might be facing us when it stopped.

The girls from the Amsterdam jail tried to talk a little to pass the time, but each of us was so overwhelmed with the not knowing that it was hard to talk about anything. We knew nothing but our misery and our fear. All the questions with no answers just took us deeper into not knowing. We finally took turns moving so one of us could sit and get some rest. Then we just rocked with the motion of the train in a mindless fog. Fear numbed all other emotions.

When I speak to groups, people ask me how we stood three days and nights on the train without going mad. I tell them that some did go mad, and that I remained sane by not being there much of the time. *I was in Zwolle, my beautiful Zwolle, helping my mother and father get ready for a very large, very important dinner. Bram, Maurits, Marthyn, and I were laughing as we helped get the room ready before the guests arrived. My brothers teased me about my reckless bike riding and asked if I ever planned to grow up and act like a young lady. I teased back by repeating, "Never, never, never". My mother would come in and out of the room to check on our progress, smile, and leave. Our father would look for something that was not being done correctly and tell us to do it right.*

I would be jolted back to the present by the movement of the train or by needing to get to the corner where we relieved ourselves. There was no privacy and no longer any shame. People near the barrel in the corner turned their heads to offer as much privacy as possible in a time and a place that had left no privacy and no dignity. Occasionally my face would feel wet, but I was never aware of crying. I had thought I had no tears left.

Parents with small children were the worst. Not only did they have to suffer hunger and thirst, but they had to watch and listen as their children begged for food and water and cried from pain and fear. There was no way to protect them from the evil that consumed all of us on every transport and in every camp. I still can't imagine what it was like for the parents, or for any who had loved ones with them and had to watch helplessly as they suffered.

I do remember that I saw countless, heartbreaking instances of selfless, sacrificial love. Parents would sit or stand in impossibly cramped positions for hours to avoid waking a sleeping child or to allow more air space for a little one; families would take turns shifting positions to give each a short time of being able to move; older couples just huddled where they could and held each other. People did everything in their power to help those they loved as long as they could.

I never saw my uncle or any of his family again after we arrived at Sobibor.

CHAPTER 10

Transport Process

Prisoners of the Third Reich came from every part of German-occupied Europe. Jews, Slavs, Russian Red Army prisoners-of-war, gypsies, homosexuals, intellectuals, the mentally or physically handicapped, political prisoners, and any non-Aryan considered a threat had to be moved to a designated labor, concentration, or death camp. The numbers involved millions, and the method for moving these people to their deaths evolved into a complex system of transports.

The box cars were packed so tightly that prisoners could only stand and perhaps make it to a bucket or low barrel in the corner or center of the car when they needed to relieve themselves. There was never food or water, and the trips could take days. Hysteria, madness, and death occurred en route. The cruelty of the transports was surpassed only by what awaited the prisoners when they were unloaded at their final destination.

Upon arrival, prisoners were selected for the showers (gas chambers) or shown their barracks if they were healthy enough to work or had needed skills. A group of prisoners who had been kept alive from previous transports were ordered to clean out the bodies of the dead or dying and the excrement that came as a result of starvation and disease. The transports were then ready for another trip.

According to meticulously kept transport records, there were nineteen trains from Westerbork to Sobibor, Poland. The numbers from each transport add up to 34,313 Dutch Jews being sent to the death camp at Sobibor. Because trains were not the only transportation bringing people to Sobibor, that number is always considered a very low estimate. These transports carried as many as could be crowded into the space, three or four times the number of people they should hold. Most were freight cars and cattle cars, not meant to carry human cargo at all. Survival rates depended on how far the trains had to travel. One German transport had taken five days to reach its destination. Ninety percent of the people on board were dead when the doors were opened.

None of the official records of Westerbork recorded the fear, or the hunger, or the cruelty of the transports. They did efficiently record the transportation of thousands for liquidation in the various camps. Westerbork kept records, but there were no records for many of the transports as the number of people being murdered and burned reached proportions that defied order or record keeping.

As stated on page vii, of the almost 35,000 or more Dutch Jews taken to Sobibor, and the 250,000 total who perished there, Selma Engel (Saartje Wijnberg) is now (in 2016) the only Dutch-born survivor.[15]

CHAPTER 11

Sobibor

On April 6, 1941, after three days and three nights of living hell, we arrived.

When the German guards slid open the doors, we fell over each other trying to get out. We were starving, crazed with not knowing our fate, and smelling death. One woman lost her baby and screamed, "My baby, my baby!" The guard told her, "We will take care of your baby." She did not see her baby again. I don't know what happened to her baby after the soldier took it, but the women with babies and small children were always the first directed toward the showers along with any elderly, sick, or crippled. To the Nazis, these people could be of no value in maintaining the camp and would only be unnecessary trouble and extra mouths to feed if kept alive.

I never personally witnessed it, but a friend of mine saw more than one baby separated from its mother, held by its heels, and bashed against a rail car. The SS officer guilty of this act on more than one occasion did stand trial and have to face witnesses. But how can justice be served for such barbaric, inhuman acts?

The soldiers told us to leave everything in a large pile, all the things that we had thought necessary to survive when we had been arrested. My backpack held little, and I tossed it on the pile with all the others. When we were left with only the clothes on our backs, they divided us. The men were herded to the left and the women to the right. I say "herded" because the whips and dogs were used freely if there was any hesitation.

Cruel, yes, but almost as sadistic was giving people baggage claim checks and telling them they could collect their luggage later, or postcards with lovely scenes of mountains to send back home with good news of the camp. The Nazis were unbelievably cruel in even small ways, but they also wanted to keep Hitler's Final Solution unknown in order to prevent panic among people in the ghettos, on the transports, and in their thousands of forced labor, concentration, and death camps.

Despite all efforts, they were unsuccessful in preventing panic among the prisoners from our transport. We were now the people in the horrifying scenes we had heard described from the small window on the train. We were now the ones screaming and begging for mercy as we had heard others do.

At first, I tried not to hear what was going on. I think I could not have remained sane if I had allowed myself to hear the cries of the mothers and children, or fully grasp what was happening. I think I went back to my old world again rather than take it all in. All of us from the Amsterdam jail tried to stay together. As we were marched past the soldiers, all healthy looking young girls, including most of us from the jail, were taken out of the line. I did not know why we had been pushed out of line. At first, I thought Ulla and I were going to experience some of the stories I had heard from the public women in the Amsterdam jail. Trying to protect her, I stepped in front of her, only to be pushed roughly to my knees and out of the way by one of the guards.

I wouldn't have worried about those of us who were pulled out of line if I had known the Nazi SS guards were too aware of their status and their superiority to rape or have sexual relations with Jews. We were treated worse than animals and referred to as dogs. They did not want to defile the blood of the Master Race with Jewish blood. We had to fear many things from the SS guards—the whips and dogs, guns, torture, and finally the gas chambers—but most were too proud of what they thought they were to rape us.

The Ukrainian guards were another story. There were cases of abuse and rape, but they were usually satisfied with the public women brought to the camp for them. The Ukrainians hated Jews and Germans almost equally, but, like all of us, they did exactly as they were told by the SS. Through it all, the Nazis looked on with their superior death-mask smiles as the gods of this insanely evil world they had created.

I think that I was spared to tell the story I am telling you now. There were too many times and too many close calls for there not to be a reason. I think Chaim and I were both spared to bear witness to the world of what hatred and prejudice created, and to share how that evil may sometimes be defeated by love and the caring acts of good people.

Those of us not sent directly to the gas chambers were told the layout of the camp and assigned jobs. We were showered and then taken to where we would live and work. We were told there was pride in work and that those who worked hard would be rewarded with extra food and clothes.

I spoke only Dutch and understood very little German, so I had to watch what others were doing and try to follow or get translations. The fear of not doing as I was told simply because I couldn't understand the orders almost paralyzed me.

The layout of the camp was simple: Camp I was where we slept, two barracks for the men and one for the women. The women's barracks had long continuous rows of rough platforms for beds and straw to be used for mattress and blanket. Ulla and I felt lucky that we got to be next to each other. Camp I was also where the prisoners with needed skills had their "shops." The tailors, boot makers, mechanics, carpenters, painters, and goldsmiths who had been saved from the gas chamber were given the equipment necessary to provide whatever was needed or wanted by the SS guards.

Camp II was where we did the work we were assigned. Luggage brought by the prisoners filled two large barracks in this camp, the results of two or three transports a week with one thousand or more prisoners on each. It amounted to mountains of every imaginable kind of suitcase, backpack, box, or bag. All were waiting to be emptied of what had once meant hope and survival. Clothes, money, and jewelry were collected, sorted, and stored in a warehouse until it could be shipped back to Germany.

We were also shown a row of neat little houses, that we learned later were for the Nazi soldiers who ran the camp. These little houses looked so normal, like a tiny Bavarian village. Unlike normal village streets, there was no talking or laughing among the people who were working on the houses or the flowers in front of each. None of the workers even looked up as we were marched by. I had missed the beautiful flowers of Zwolle while in hiding and in different jails, but these flowers did not make me feel happy as the ones in Zwolle always had.

We did not know it at the time, but Sobibor was not a concentration or forced labor camp. It was one of four death camps built to execute the Final Solution, the official policy of making Europe *Judenfrei* (Jew free). Prisoners were brought here for the sole purpose of being slaughtered as quickly and efficiently as possible. Many years later I learned that Sobibor was known as the most advanced and most efficient of the four death camps in carrying out this plan. Only those needed to do the work of the camp were saved from the gas chambers. Being saved from the gas chamber was temporary, until the prisoners became sick, too weak to work, or caught the attention of the wrong guard; they then joined all the others who had been sent to the gas chamber.

The North Camp was outside the barbed wire barriers surrounding the camp. Here trees were cut and stones were hauled to do what building was needed in the camp and to create impossibly difficult work for the prisoners. Because the work was designed to punish as much as to be productive, the North Camp was responsible for many punishments and deaths. Prisoners would be ordered to lift impossibly heavy logs or roll huge stones. When they could not do as ordered, they were cruelly whipped. Other prisoners were not allowed to help, and this created another kind of punishment for all who had to watch and could only stand by helplessly. Severe beatings meant being sent to Camp III if the prisoner could no longer work.

Camp III was where the showers were, where we were gassed by the thousands. The Camp III workers had their own barracks and were never allowed to come in contact with the other prisoners. Like baggage claim checks given to many when they were told to leave their luggage on the unloading platform and the speeches telling us we had nothing to fear if we worked hard, the German guards thought that separating the Camp III workers from the rest of us kept the unbelievable horror of what went on there just a rumor.

Camp IV was where the sorted clothes and valuables were packed and stored to be shipped back to Germany.

My first impressions of Sobibor were horrifyingly mixed. Some things, like the little houses, seemed normal. But everything else contradicted that. We still hoped for the best, but the watchtowers manned by armed guards and the multiple strands of barbed wire surrounding the camp and the haunted, hopeless faces of the people we saw were far from any normal I had ever known.

The work I was assigned at Camp II was sorting clothes. When I first saw two large barracks filled with tables overflowing with luggage of every size and shape, I felt lucky to have this job instead of one of the harder ones. I didn't know at the time that the owners of the suitcases and backpacks had already been sent to the gas chambers in Camp III, or how the contents of that luggage would eventually come to affect me. The instructions we were given were specific. Again, I had to get orders translated for me by one of the other prisoners who understood German. We were ordered to sort everything into piles of "first quality" and "second quality." We were to search for papers, money, jewelry, and anything else that might have value. To the Germans, everything had value. Gold was taken from teeth, and women on their way to the gas chamber had their hair cut so it could be used to make felt for winter boots. Nothing was wasted but the lives of the prisoners.

Before sending these valuables back to Germany, the Nazi soldiers kept so much for themselves that when they went on leave every few weeks, their cars were piled high with things that had been brought to the camps by the prisoners. I later learned that many Nazis volunteered for camp duty. The opportunity to scavenge the valuables of a murdered people was one of the reasons for volunteering. The opportunity to exercise unlimited power and unleash inhuman cruelty, with no restraints, was another reason for the most brutal guards volunteering.

As we were told how to sort the clothes and what to do with stored food and valuables, we were also warned repeatedly that the penalty for trying to steal anything for ourselves was immediate death.

Five o'clock every night was time for daily roll call. After everyone was accounted for, we had to do whatever the Germans decided would amuse them. Often, there were punishments to be dealt out—tortures, whippings, executions. Twenty-five lashes were given for not working fast enough or just for being noticed by the wrong guard; to the cook for not being able to serve bread and soup to six hundred prisoners in twenty minutes; to those working in the North Camp for not being able to lift the trees that had been cut. Sometimes we just walked and ran for hours, around and around the camp. Sometimes we did calisthenics to the point of exhaustion. Whatever the orders, the roll-call activities were not only entertainment for the guards but also ways of weeding out those who were getting too weak to work. The Nazis didn't waste food on prisoners who were not strong enough to work.

CHAPTER 12

Sobibor's Dark History

With her arrival at Sobibor, Saartje Wijnberg became one of the victims of the Final Solution. Sobibor had been constructed as one of the three extermination camps, along with Belzec and Treblinka, to carry out Operation Reinhard, created to achieve the Final Solution as established at the Wannsee Conference of 1942. Chelmno is often included as one of the death camps, although it was not originally constructed strictly for the extermination of Jews.

Not only had Saartje Wijnberg become a part of the Final Solution, she had arrived at the death camp known as the most efficient camp in its killing procedures. Sobibor was the second death camp to be constructed and was patterned after Belzec, the first to be tested and become fully operational. Based on lessons learned, Belzec served as a model for the other death camps being constructed and as a training site for top SS personnel assigned to Sobibor.

In early 1942, the Germans began their plans for Sobibor. After surveillance from the air, two SS officers arrived by train to assess the area on foot. Engineer SS Obersturm*Fuehrer* Wolfgang Richard Thomalla was the construction expert for Operation Reinhard, and with him was the construction supervisor for Sobibor, General Hilmar Moser. After walking the area and taking specific measurements, Thomalla and Moser felt they had the perfect location for the second death camp. The chosen site was in a remote area twenty five miles north of Chelm, Poland, near the village of Sobibor (Forest of the Owls) and the Chelm-Wlodawa railway line. Approximately three miles from the Bug River, this swampy, densely-wooded area afforded the easy rail access needed for importing large numbers of prisoners from other camps and holding sites. The use of trucks to import prisoners had proved too slow when used at Chelmno, as had the methods of gassing and disposing of bodies. The remoteness of the site for Sobibor death camp supported the planned secrecy of the camp and provided the opportunity to improve on prior methods of gassing and body disposal.

By March of 1942, a new spur and a concrete ramp had been added to the existing Chelm-Wlodawa rail line. The additions were inside the camp, behind a fence heavily woven with pine branches. This created an area that was invisible to the people of this Lublin district of Poland or any rail passengers whose destination was not the unloading platform inside the camp.

The initial construction of the camp was done by eighty Jews brought from nearby ghettos; all were shot when the first phase was completed. The secrecy of Sobibor and its purpose had to be maintained in order for the mission of this and the other death camps to be completed—the rapid, efficient extermination and body disposal of all Jews transported by rail from all over Europe. By April, the camp was completed, and the first prisoners were unloaded from the transports as soon as the gas chambers had been tested.[16]

Surrounded by a triple-strand barbed wire fence, trees planted to obscure the site, and later a 50-foot-wide mine field, the camp covered an area of approximately 1,312 by 1,969 feet. Nine watchtowers, manned by Ukrainian guards, were spaced around the perimeter with a high observation tower overlooking the entire area.

As described by Saartje, Lager I (Camp I) was the SS administration area, the workshops of the Jews saved from gassing because they possessed special skills needed by the SS: tailors, cobblers, one for the SS officers and one for the Ukrainian guards, carpenters, blacksmiths, painters, and goldsmiths. Camp I also included the barracks and the kitchen for Jewish prisoners.

The barracks were made of rough wood, approximately 70 by 40 feet, and housed two hundred women and four hundred men. The number fluctuated as prisoners died from malnutrition, illness, punishments, or gassing and had to be replaced by those saved from incoming transports to do the work needed by the SS to run the camp.[17] Inside the barracks, three levels of rough platforms were used for beds, and prisoners used whatever they could find to cover themselves. The toilet was a pail placed in the middle of the room.

Camp II was the reception area where incoming transports unloaded as many as two to three thousand people at least once a day at the height of the camp's operation. Those who had survived the horror of the transport now found themselves being directed: women and children to the right, men to the left. Women with children, the elderly, and the sick were sent directly to the gas chamber. Incoming prisoners first had to surrender all belongings and wait to be "selected" for the showers or for the work details. If selected for the showers, they were herded to Camp III where they were ordered to strip or be stripped, have their hair cut, and then they were driven into the showers. Those who were chosen for their needed skills or for their little remaining strength and good health, were shown their barracks and ordered to line up for work assignments.

Camp III was the top secret section of Sobibor, with great effort put into denying and concealing its existence. Even the prisoners were not to know what lay beyond the corridor of trees called the Tube. There were rumors, but any who ventured too close to Camp III, the extermination and cremation site for Sobibor, never returned. The prisoners who had to do the work of Camp III were never allowed to mix with the other prisoners, so rumors were rarely supported with proof of what went on in Camp III.

Originally, there were three gas chambers at Sobibor, with a capacity for 160-180 prisoners each. With an increase in the number of incoming transports in 1942, and in the number of prisoners on each transport (as many as five thousand at the height of the operation), faster extermination methods for the prisoners and for disposing of their bodies had to be developed. The construction of new gas chambers increased the rate of extermination to 1300 prisoners at one time. [18]

The staff at Sobibor consisted of from 20-30 SS officers and from 90-120 guards, most of whom were Ukrainian. All ninety-six SS officers chosen to run the death camps had been active at euthanasia centers prior to being transferred to the death camps. All non-SS guards were trained at an SS facility in Lublin, Poland, the Trawniki Training Camp. The site and the personnel had been chosen carefully for the task at hand, and they were horrifyingly proficient.[19]

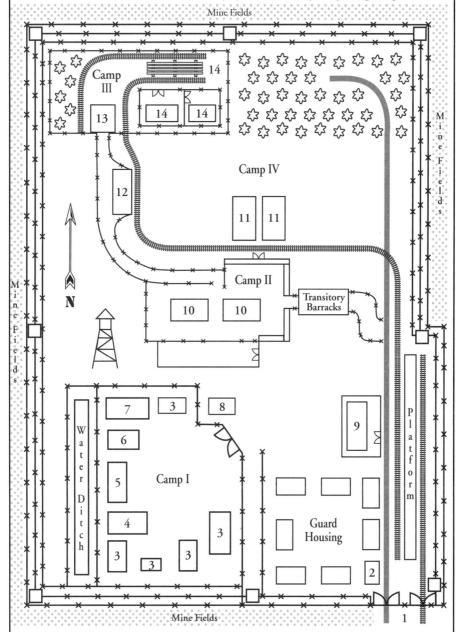

MAP OF SOBIBOR DEATH CAMP
Based on research and the memory of Selma (Saartje Wijnberg) Engel

Mine Fields

Mine Fields

Mine Fields

Mine Fields

Camp III

14

14   14

13

Camp IV

12

11   11

N

Camp II

10   10

Transitory Barracks

Water Ditch

7   3   8

6

5

Camp I

4

3   3

3

3

9

Platform

Guard Housing

2

1

Mine Fields

1.) Main entrance
2.) Sentry box, housing for guards - German and Ukrainian
3.) Tailor, shoe maker, goldsmith, jeweler, painter, carpenter - for SS guards & officers
4 & 5.) Barracks for male prisoners
6.) Kitchen
7.) Barracks for female prisioners

8.) Toilet
9.) SS Officers' House
10.) Sorting sheds for victims' (victims' luggage)
11.) Storage sheds for victims' belongings
12.) Barracks where Jewish women had heads shorn before entering gas chambers
13.) Gas chambers
14.) Crematorium - Camp III workers barracks

Heinrich Himmler
In charge of SS, responsible for all
concentration, labor, and death camps

Franz Stangl
Sobibor's First Commandant

Gustav Wagner
Considered the most brutal of the
Sobibor SS guards

Karl Frenzel
In charge of Camp I at Sobibor

Key Personnel responsible for Sobibor Death Camp

CHAPTER 13

Our First Dance

I remember one special night of my first week at Sobibor more clearly than I remember yesterday. This was the night my life was changed forever. That night the SS guards had decided there were to be no punishments. They wanted entertainment, so some of the prisoners were told they were going to attend a party. A few musicians, who had been saved from Camp III to provide music when the guards wanted it, were ordered to play dance music for this party.

It was a cold, clear, early spring night. The SS guards not on duty stood at the edge of the roll call area, laughing and smoking, pointing at first one of us, then another. I thought they were deciding which prisoners were to dance and with whom, but I didn't understand them. We all stood in line, waiting to be told our next move, or to be shot or whipped for no reason.

The musicians who had been ordered to play began to tune their instruments. The rest of us waited to see what would come next. We never knew. It often depended on a whim of one of the guards or an order not being obeyed by one of the prisoners. If ordered to dance, even if too sick or too weak, we still had to obey the order or join all the others who had gone to Camp III. The musicians began to play. I don't remember the music that was played, but I do remember thinking it was good that something of such beauty could still exist, even here in the midst of such ugliness and death.

Suddenly, words rang out, "Sie! Tanz mit dem Polen." I heard them, but I didn't understand them. The words were repeated, more loudly and harshly, with the handle of a whip pointed at me, "Sie, Niederlanderin!

Tanz mit dem Polen!" I understood only the word, "Dutch," and panicked, trying to figure out how to follow the order. Expecting a blow from the whip or worse, I bowed my head and waited. At that moment, the same SS officer pointed his whip handle at someone behind me and shouted, "Sie! Tanz mit dem Niederlanderin!"

Suddenly in front of me stood a pair of dusty boots, and a soft voice spoke words I did not understand. Daring to raise my head, I looked into the kind eyes of a handsome young Polish man I had noticed before. He had an air of quiet confidence and control in spite of the constant horrors of this time and place. He smiled, took my hand gently in his, and led me to where we were supposed to dance together. When I hadn't understood the order, they had then ordered this man to dance with me. My heart still speaks to me, and I smile when I think of that night and my first dance with Chaim.

The musicians continued to play, and as we moved together to the music, I had a feeling I had never had with any other dance partner. It was as if I belonged here in this man's arms even though I did not know his name and had heard him speak only words I did not understand. It was as if, in spite of everything surrounding us, I was safe here.

Chaim told everybody, as long as he lived, that the moment he took me in his arms that night, he fell instantly in love with me. By the end of our first dance, he was more determined than ever to survive the hell of Sobibor and to save me as well. For me it took a little longer, but I fell just as deeply in love with him and dared to hope that there would be an end to this brutal world that was ruled by dehumanizing punishments and death. In spite of the horrors of this place, the whole world seemed suddenly full of possibilities. Hopes and dreams again filled me with a happiness that I had forgotten ever existed.

I wanted the dance to go on forever. But when the guards had tired of their entertainment for the evening, they stopped the musicians and dismissed all of us from the party. Chaim held my hand firmly in his until we reached my barracks. Then the look in his eyes told me that, in spite of the drifting ash and the smells from the fires, in spite of the hunger and the fear, in spite of everything that had gone before and that now surrounded us, this night was a new beginning for both of us.

After our meeting at the dance, we never had a minute of privacy. When we could speak to each other, we whispered of freedom and our dream of surviving to share a normal life. This dream that grew from our love gave us hope to cling to when there seemed to be nothing left.

Chaim spoke Polish, German, and Yiddish; I spoke only Dutch and understood a few German words. In the little time we had together, we taught each other our languages and told each other our stories. Amazingly, we were always able to understand each other in spite of the language differences. I thought then, and I know now, that love has its own language, one that makes understanding possible even without words. At this time I was twenty, Chaim was twenty six, and neither of us had ever been in love before. Now we were both sure, and we promised each other that no matter what happened, we would face it together and survive.

CHAPTER 14

Dreams Amid Horrors

Chaim had been at Sobibor eleven months and before that in the Polish Army. He had been captured and sent to a German prisoner-of-war camp and then to Sobibor, so he knew about surviving. He was quiet, but had an air of control and strength about him. Quiet confidence was a part of his nature, but it was supported by a toughness that had been brought to full strength by what he had already been through and survived.

We were never apart after that moment at the dance except to do our assigned work during the day and go to our separate barracks at night. We were never alone together, but our love was so obvious that even the guards laughingly called us the bride and groom. The other women in the barracks teased me by saying that Chaim guarded me like fresh butter.

We were fearful of being noticed. One of the rules for survival at Sobibor was to remain invisible, never to attract attention. Any glance, any word, any wrong move could be misinterpreted by a guard, and life ended on a whim. But we did not know how to hide this love that had given us hope and our dream of surviving. Without Chaim I would never have made it out of Sobibor or lived through the months that followed. He taught me how to be invisible by keeping my head down and avoiding eye contact with the guards. He helped me pick lice from my blanket. He made me eat, no matter how terrible the food was. He took care of me when I was delirious with typhus. I still don't know how he saved me from the gas chamber, which was the fate of all who were sick or weak.

I had nothing to give but my love, but it must have been enough. He always said that without my love, he would not have been so determined to survive the atrocities of Sobibor and live to share a normal life with me.

We knew the penalty for theft of any kind—we had been forced to watch the tortures and executions at many roll calls—but we stole food anyway. One young boy was shot for taking a single tin of sardines, but taking the risk was better than starving or getting too weak to work. The work in the sorting sheds gave us the opportunity to go through all luggage, backpacks, or bundles the prisoners had brought with them. Most had packed items of food—cheeses, bread, small tins of ham—to help them survive. We became very skillful at dropping one item while hiding another in our clothes when we bent over to pick up what we had dropped. As dangerous as it was to steal food, we had no choice if we were going to survive. And we were determined to survive.

Chaim said I was much better and braver at stealing food than he was, but I just had more room in my clothes to hide things. I could hide bread or a chocolate bar or small tins of food in my bra or underpants and never be searched, so I stole all the food I could. We shared the food I stole with my cousin Elly Nathan and our friends Ulla and Minnie Katz.

When Chaim worked in the sorting shed, he took anything that might be of value in paying our way to freedom after we escaped Sobibor. He never doubted that we would survive and have a life beyond Sobibor; so he took gold, money, diamonds, jewelry, anything we might exchange for food or shelter. We told no one of the money and valuables Chaim was risking his life to steal and bury in a hole under the ashes of the blacksmith's fire. We knew well the penalty for stealing food or anything of value, but we also knew we could be beaten or shot by the guards for any reason, or for no reason. We also knew we could not survive a hostile Polish countryside after an escape without money and valuables to pay for food and shelter, so we had no choice. Even now I am amazed that Chaim and I were not caught and shot for stealing.

One morning on the way to my job in Camp II, I saw a man from Zwolle and tried to get his attention, "Hi, it's me, Saartje Wijnberg from the hotel!" I called to him a second time, but he never answered. His head stayed down, and he walked past as if he hadn't heard me. He had been

the cantor from our temple; I never saw him again. I later learned from
Chaim the danger of attracting attention in any way; I knew then why the
man hadn't answered me.

Through the horrors and our struggle to survive another day, the skies
turned red, the fires burned, and the sickeningly sweet smell became a
part of everything. The transport trains were bringing prisoners so fast
that burying the bodies, even in mass graves, was not efficient enough.
Burning the bodies was faster and left less evidence of what was happening at Sobibor, so the fires burned longer and brighter.

A few days later, another man from Zwolle found me when there were
no guards near and offered us a chance to join a planned escape. His wife
and child had been killed as soon as they had arrived at Sobibor. Now he
had heard that some Dutch prisoners were planning to escape, and he was
going to join them. He had no reason not to, and he felt someone had to
tell the world what was happening. I could only wish him luck.

Chaim and I had decided to wait until the time seemed right for
someone to lead the whole camp out. So many had tried alone or in small
groups, and they were always caught, brought back, and lined up for punishment at roll call as warning for the rest of us.

A German Jew informed the SS of the Dutch plans, thinking mis-
takenly that he could get special favors, so the man from Zwolle and the
others were caught trying to escape. In retaliation, the SS guards lined up
seventy-two Dutch men and boys at roll call and shot them in front of the
whole camp. Some had not even known of the escape plan, but guilt and
innocence meant nothing for Germans when dealing with Jews. The bodies of the seventy-two Dutch men and boys, as with all murdered prisoners, were thrown carelessly on a trolley and taken to be burned.

One time, for reasons that only the SS guards knew, they lined up
every man in the camp and shot every tenth man. My Chaim was number
nine that night. By the end of that roll call, there was no sound from the
several hundred prisoners who were, as always, made to observe the punishments and executions. I was so tense from trying to figure out where

the count was, and where Chaim was standing, that I almost fainted when the guard doing the counting passed him as number nine, and shot the man standing next to him between the eyes.

Stories that I heard told from prisoners of other camps after the liberation were as unbelievably horrible as the ones from Sobibor. In one camp, I don't remember which one now, one of the guards, a former boxer, bragged that he had created a special whip that could kill a Jew with twelve lashes. He also bragged that his record was eight lashes for a small Jew.

Another guard, I believe it was at a different camp, had trained his huge dog to respond to his command of, "Man, get the dog!" by attacking the genitals or buttocks of any man who needed punishment for any reason, or just for the entertainment of the guard. After such an attack, the prisoner was no longer able to work, so Camp III was next. How can a normal mind and heart and soul observe these things and remain sane?

The entire camp population was forced to watch all punishments. Observing was meant not only to deter us from stealing food or trying to escape, but also to remind us that we were not considered human. There are no words to describe the brutality, the cruelty, and the constant degradation. We never knew who would be next.

During the punishments I always found Chaim or he found me. He stood beside me, held my hand tightly, and told me to keep my head up but my eyes closed. He told me to think beyond this time to our life together when we escaped. We couldn't look down or we would join those being punished, or, even worse, have to administer the punishment.

Chaim's first job, after arriving on a cattle car, full of prisoners but with no food or water, had been to sort through the suitcases and clothes of those sent to the gas chamber. From his transport of more than a thousand, eighteen were pulled aside and assigned work. While sorting clothes into the first quality and second quality piles, he found his brother's bloody clothes with all the family pictures in the pockets. His mother, Frieda, had died when he was sixteen; now his brother was gone, and Chaim discovered later that his father had also died at Sobibor. He could show no emotion and there was no time to grieve, so he resisted the only way he could: by damaging as many things as he could to destroy their value for the Germans, and by stealing anything that could help us survive.

By now, we had all heard rumors about what was really happening at the other camps, but it was so unacceptable, so beyond what we could comprehend, that we found it hard to believe. How could the horror we were living through exist anywhere else? We had no idea of the scope of the extermination plans for the Jews and others who did not approve of Hitler's insane plans. Only later did we learn of the four death camps and of Operation Reinhard that made complete annihilation of all Jews official policy and top priority.

Surviving at Sobibor meant not only trying to be invisible but eating food that the dogs of the SS guards would not eat. Their dogs ate well; the food for the prisoners was unbelievable, almost impossible to eat. The soup was like boiled straw, the bread looked and tasted like clay, and the coffee was just brown water. It was always the same, except for what we risked our lives to steal.

Chaim called me brave, but I was really like a little mouse, frightened all the time and unable to sleep many nights because of dreams of my mother and brothers and fear of what was to become of us. After a while, I caught part of Chaim's courage and determination to survive, and I stopped being frightened all the time.

The work that almost destroyed my Chaim and threatened to make him forget our promises to each other was when he was assigned to cut the hair of the women before they entered the gas chamber. To refuse would have meant immediate death, but to obey destroyed a part of him that was never recovered. He could never talk of the depth of this horror, of the cries of those women, or of the look in their eyes without feeling overwhelming guilt at the price paid for our escape and eventual freedom. A part of my husband walked into the gas chamber and died with each one of them.

Some of the women did not realize what was happening and thought they were just being showered and deloused before being assigned work. Others realized what the showers really were and, naked, shivering, clinging to their children, begged for their lives but even more for the lives of their children. Chaim was a good man, and their cries for mercy, and their desperate begging for the lives of their children haunted his nightmares the rest of his life.

We feared all the guards, but Wagner was the worst of the Nazis. He was huge—6'4" and 240 pounds—and evil. He was only twenty-eight or thirty, and very bright, very cunning. He stalked around the compound like a predatory animal sniffing for prey. He was aware of even the most inconsequential change in surroundings or in any of the prisoners. It was as if he could sense something in the air before it was evident to anyone else. We knew we had to be extraordinarily careful of everything when he was around; it was the time to become invisible. We also knew no escape could succeed while he was in camp.

One train brought a group to Sobibor from Bergen-Belsen. When the transport doors opened, they tried to resist and were shot immediately. When Chaim sorted their bloody clothes, a note in one of the pockets read simply, "Take Revenge." We did what we could. We ate their garbage, we stole food, we destroyed what we could in the sorting sheds, and those prisoners who had not given up hope planned escapes. One of the kapos, a German Jew, took his position of power seriously and caused many deaths by reporting on his own people in exchange for better food and promised survival. He even wanted those who were kept alive for maintaining the camp to have numbers tattooed on their arms. A Jewish medic gave him something to make him sick, and then he was beaten to death so it wouldn't show how he died. Nothing was ever suspected or the guilty and the innocent would have suffered for it. I think the Germans didn't really care how he died, just one more dead Jew. A few prisoners who could take no more, openly defied the Germans and were immediately shot, or brutalized and then shot.

Through all this horror, the transports continued to come two or three times a day with a thousand or more people arriving each time. The fires continued to light the night sky, and we clung with a fierce strength born of desperation to our hopes and dreams of someday having a normal life together.

CHAPTER 15

Sobibor Personnel

Although the plans for the systematic extermination of the Jews of Europe were based on Hitler's early anti-Semitism and his later need for an arch-enemy to unite the German people, the Wannsee Conference of 1942 laid down the plans for the Final Solution. While the vision and the plans were the creation of Nazi leadership, the day-to-day perpetrators were willing, enthusiastic, and brutally efficient in executing their jobs.

SS Obersturmfuehrer (Senior Storm Leader) Franz Stangl served as the first Kommandant of Sobibor. Born in Austria in 1908, Stangl was reared as a Catholic, became a master weaver, and taught himself to play the zither well enough to give lessons. Nothing in his early life or accomplishments foreshadowed his ultimate depravity.[20]

Recognized as an efficient administrator, Stangl, by direct order from Heinrich Himmler, head of the SS, became superintendent of the Euthanasia Programme at Euthanasia Institute at Schloss Hartheim in 1940. From here, he was transferred in March of 1942 to Poland to manage Operation Reinhard under Odilo Globocnik. After serving as Sobibor's first Kommandant for six months, Stangl was transferred to assume the same position at Treblinka.[21] Franz Stangl's time at Sobibor was short, from March to September, 1942, but the impact of his organization and efficiency was felt until the camp was destroyed after the escape.

Author Gitta Sereny conducted an interview with Stangl in 1970, which later appeared in her book, *Into That Darkness: An Examination of Conscience*, published in 1983. This interview shows the depths to which Franz Stangl had descended as Kommandant of Sobibor.

"Would it be true to say that you got used to the liquidations?"

He thought for a moment, "To tell you the truth," he then said, slowly and thoughtfully, "one did become used to it."

"In days? Weeks? Months?"

"Months. It was months before I could look one of them in the eye. I repressed it all by trying to create a special place: gardens, new barracks, new kitchens, new everything; barbers, tailors, shoemakers, carpenters. There were hundreds of ways to take one's mind off it; I used them all."

"Even so, if you felt that strongly, there had to be times, perhaps at night, in the dark, when you couldn't avoid thinking about it?"

"In the end, the only way to deal with it was to drink. I took a large glass of brandy to bed with me each night and I drank."

"I think you are evading my question."

"No, I don't mean to; of course, thoughts came. But I forced them away. I made myself concentrate on work, work and again work."

"Would it be true to say that you finally felt they weren't really human beings?"

"When I was on a trip once, years later in Brazil," he said, his face deeply concentrated, and obviously reliving the experience, "my train stopped next to a slaughterhouse. The cattle in the pens hearing the noise of the train, trotted up to the fence and stared at the train. They were very close to my window, one crowding the other, looking at me through that fence. I thought then, 'Look at this, this reminds me of Poland; that's just how the people looked, trustingly, just before they went into the tins…'"

"You said tins," I interrupted. "What do you mean?" But he went on without hearing or answering me.

"…I couldn't eat tinned meat after that. Those big eyes which looked at me not knowing that in no time at all they'd all be dead." He paused. His face was drawn. At this moment he looked old and worn and real.

"So you didn't feel they were human beings?"

"Cargo," he said tonelessly. "they were cargo." He raised and dropped his hand in a gesture of despair. Both our voices had dropped. It was one of the few times in those weeks of talks that he made no effort to cloak his despair, and his hopeless grief allowed a moment of sympathy.

"When do you think you began to think of them as cargo? The way you spoke earlier, of the day when you first came to Treblinka, the horror you felt seeing the dead bodies everywhere—they weren't 'cargo' to you then, were they?"

"I think it started the day I first saw the *Totenlager* in Treblinka. I remember Wirth standing there, next to the pits full of blue-black corpses. It had nothing to do with humanity, it couldn't have; it was a mass – a mass of rotting flesh. Wirth said, 'What shall we do with this garbage?' I think unconsciously that started me thinking of them as cargo."

"There were so many children, did they ever make you think of your children, of how you would feel in the position of those parents?"

"No," he said slowly, "I can't think I ever thought that way. "He paused. "You see," he then continued, still speaking with this extreme seriousness and obviously intent on finding new truth within himself, "I rarely saw them as individuals. It was always a huge mass. I sometimes stood on the wall and saw them in the tube. But how can I explain it—they were naked, packed together, running, being driven with whips like..." the sentence trailed off.

"Could you not have changed that?" I asked. "In your position, could you not have stopped the nakedness, the whips, the horror of the cattle pens?"

"No, no, no. This was the system. Wirth had invented it. It worked and because it worked, it was irreversible."[22]

Another Austrian, Franz Reichleitner, called The Idiot by the prisoners, was the second and final Kommandant of Sobibor Death Camp. Prior to Sobibor, Reichleitner had served with the Gestapo in Linz, Germany. After a visit by Himmler to Sobibor on February 12, 1943, Reichleitner was promoted to *SS HauptsturmFuehrer* (Chief Storm Leader).[23]

In spite of his rank and assigned position as Kommandant, Reichleitner was rarely seen by the prisoners, but the camp was run even more strictly and brutally than it had been under Stangl's command because Gustav Wagner was placed in charge.

SS OberscharFuehrer (Senior Leader) Gustav Wagner was well known to the prisoners and remembered for his large size, his bellowing voice, but even more for his unpredictable rages played out in indiscriminate attacks with fists, baton, whip, or pistol. Called The Beast by the prisoners, he stated in a 1979 BBC interview, "I had no feelings. It just became another job. In the evening we never discussed our work but just drank and played cards."[24]

Wagner was in charge of incoming transports and followed the same procedure with each arrival. Backed by other SS officers, guards, and kapos, all personnel armed, and with dogs barking and lunging at their leashes, Wagner screamed his orders as the prisoners, wild with hunger and thirst and fear, jumped off the cars.

"Austreten von den Waggonen!"

"Kinder links! Frauen links!" (Women and children left.) They were taken directly to the showers. As Wagner bellowed his orders, the kapos stood ready to enforce them. A few women and healthy-looking men were polled for needed skills and taken to the barracks in Camp I instead of being directed to the showers in Camp III.

Wagner was also credited with having a kind of sixth sense about the prisoners and could sense anything out of the ordinary. Many of the prisoners felt the escape they had planned and executed could not have happened if Wagner had not been on leave.

Karl August Wilhelm Frenzel was in charge of Camp I from his arrival at Sobibor on April 20, 1942, through the time of the escape on October 14, 1943. Prior to his time at Sobibor, Frenzel had been a guard at Euthanasienstalt Grafence and had helped plan gas chambers in Hadaman. He, like all the SS men, was well prepared for the work he was assigned to do. In spite of numerous documented instances of brutality, including holding a baby by its feet and swinging its head against the side of a rail car, Frenzel stated, "I feel I am justified in saying, I was well-liked by the Jews."[25]

The Ukrainian guards numbered about two hundred at any given time and were responsible for guarding the main gate, the perimeter, and the watch towers. They carried out the German orders for executions unless the SS officers killed in a fit of rage or decided for no known reason to punish or kill a prisoner. These guards hated their German masters but surpassed them in cruelty to impress them with their loyalty. Armed with whips and captured Russian carbines, the guards were used but never trusted by the SS officers and were allowed to carry only a few cartridges for their rifles when on duty. They were not allowed to keep their rifles with them while off duty.

With the Kommandant currently assigned to Sobibor, well-trained and armed SS officers with their dogs, kapos, and Ukrainian guards desperate to please their German masters, the planning and execution of the escape from Sobibor stands as an example of a rebellion that succeeded in spite of the brutal efficiency of the death camp personnel.

CHAPTER 16

Escape Plans

One transport in September of 1943 carried a group of Russian soldiers from Minsk and with them what was to be the key for escape for the whole camp. The Russians wanted to escape their first day but were talked into waiting until a plan could be made for the whole camp to escape. They were told about failed escape plans, how many had been caught and killed, and that no help would come from the population around the camp after an escape. Most Polish people hated Jews as much as they hated Germans, and killed them for the rewards from the Germans or for the money and jewels that the Poles thought all Jews carried. The Russians were told of two who had succeeded in their escape and of the thirteen men and boys who had not been involved, but who were shot at roll call to pay for the escape of those two. If the Russians did escape, they would then be on their own in unfamiliar, hostile territory with men and dogs after them and nowhere to hide or look for help. The Russians agreed to wait.

Their leader, Lieutenant Alexander Pechersky, or Sasha to his men, had been in German prisoner-of-war or labor camps for almost two years. When it was discovered that he was circumcised and therefore a Jew, he received the death sentence of being sent to Sobibor. Even after two years of brutality and deprivation, Sasha Pechersky was Russian Red Army and proud of it. He remained defiant, but he was smart about it and refused to cringe before either the Ukrainian guards, the kapos, or the SS guards. The Russian soldiers were trained, battle hardened, and tough enough, with Sasha's leadership, to have survived other camps and still enter Sobibor marching in rank with heads held high.

We watched as they were marched into the camp, bringing our hope for escape with them. Unless prisoners had given up all hope, they dreamed of escape and whispered of it to those they could trust. Many whispered plans to Leon Feldhendler, the son of a rabbi, who had earned the respect and trust of all who knew him. He was quiet, courageous, and always fair in dealing with prisoners and guards. Everyone listened to him. He knew that with the transports going from one or two a week in the spring of 1943, to none by fall, that the time for escape had come. If there were no trains bringing people to the gas chambers, there was no reason to keep Sobibor open. It would be time for those of us who had been kept alive to do the work of the camp to join all who had gone to Camp III before us. He also felt that the arrival of the Russian soldiers, with Alexander Pechersky as their leader, could make the long-dreamed-of-escape for the entire camp possible.

Before any plans could be discussed, he had to be sure the Russian soldiers in general, and Sasha Pechersky in particular, could be trusted. Feldhendler set up a casual meeting with Pechersky, and the two men felt almost immediately that they could trust each other. Their very different backgrounds were not as important as the kind of man each was. Both were strong, experienced, and had earned the respect and loyalty of all who had been involved with them. They realized that any chance of a successful escape depended on a detailed plan and total secrecy until the time of the actual escape. Only the few directly involved in the planning and execution of specific jobs could know of the plans.

I knew nothing. Chaim knew more, but just concerning his part in the plan. He said nothing to me about the escape until the day it was to take place. We would face two fences of barbed wire, mines planted in the fields around the camp, armed guards in nine or ten watchtowers and brutal retaliation if the plot was discovered.

So Leon Feldhendler, son of a Polish rabbi, and Sergeant Alexander Pechersky of the Russian Red Army became co-planners and co-leaders of what was to be the largest escape from any Nazi camp. Leon deferred to Sasha's military training and experience in the planning, and Sasha deferred to Leon's knowledge of the camp, the prisoners, and the guards in the execution of the plan.

I still marvel that these two men, with all their knowledge and experience and toughness, came together at exactly the time the prisoners of Sobibor had only weeks to live unless they escaped. They met, and each was willing to put his own life and the life of every prisoner in the hands of the other.

CHAPTER 17

The Escape

On the day of the escape, Chaim told me to say nothing to anyone, to wear as many warm clothes as I could put on and still run, and to wear good boots. I was to be ready at 3:00 for whatever the next step was.

The time for the escape was set for October 13, 1943, but a group of SS officers appeared unexpectedly at the camp, so the plans had to be changed. After the SS left the camp, the escape was set for the next day, October 14, 1943, no matter what occurred. We could delay no longer.

I was sick with worry. Would I be risking Chaim's life by going? He said he would not leave without me, so I knew I had to do my best. I had been sick with typhus and was still so weak that I was afraid I would not be strong enough to keep up. Chaim said this might be our only chance for freedom, and he felt it was far better to die trying than to remain and be shot or beaten to death for something we had not done.

Years later I learned of the courage and careful planning that had made the success of the escape possible. By the time Chaim told me to get ready to meet him, the telephone lines had already been cut, the generator was out of commission, and eleven SS guards had been enticed to appointments for boot fittings, trying on new leather coats, anything that would appeal to them, and then, one by one, had been killed by the people who were a part of the plan. The plotters used axes and knives that had been made and hidden by the blacksmith. As each officer was attacked, sawdust or blankets were used to cover the blood so the murders would remain secret as long as possible. The longer we had before the guards knew of the escape plans, the greater our chances of surviving.

We were to line up at the whistle for roll call and then begin to march out the front gate as if on late work detail for the North Camp. Although most kapos could not be trusted, two who could be had been included in the plan. These two were to march us toward the front gate and through it as part of a normal routine to give us a chance to make it to the forest before the machine guns in the towers started. Chaim told me where to wait for him in front of the medicine shed, to be there at 3:30 this time, but to wait until he came. I was there at 3:30, staying close to the building to be less visible.

Trying to appear normal, I waited, heart pounding, breath coming hard and fast. Was I doing the right thing by trying to go? I knew Chaim meant it when he said he wouldn't escape without me. I wouldn't take his chance for freedom away; and even if we didn't make it, at least we were trying and would die together. It must have been only a few minutes before I saw Chaim enter the Administration Building with two others. A few seconds or minutes later I heard muffled screams. Who had screamed? The scream didn't sound like Chaim, but I couldn't be sure.

When I saw Chaim run out the door, my heart beat even harder, but this time from joy and relief. My Chaim was alive and coming to get me! Covered in blood, he tried to catch his breath as he told me he had stabbed a guard, Beckmann, when the man who was supposed to kill him couldn't do it at the last minute. Chaim said he had shouted at Beckmann as he stabbed him over and over, "For my father! For my brother! For all the Jews you killed!"

I desperately tried to wipe the blood from his face and hands and jacket. A torn handkerchief was all I had to bind the deep cuts on his hand and wrist. I just kept saying, "Oh, my God! My God! Chaim! Chaim!"

At that moment, a whistle sounded. We knew it had to be the signal for our last roll call and the race for the forest.

Chaim grabbed my hand, held it tightly and whispered, "Come, Selma."

We ran with all the others desperate to escape the hell of Sobibor. Through the first gate, down the corridor, stumbling, waiting for machine guns from the watchtowers to cut us down, running as hard as we could, not thinking, just running for the safety of the forest. We could hear shooting from pistols and the rapid fire of machine guns, shouts and screams and people falling all around us. We just kept running, jumping over those who fell in front of us.

We reached the forest and continued to run, not knowing where we were or where we were going. We knew if we could reach the forest as darkness came, we would at least have a chance of making it through our first night. We ran until I could run no more. I had to stop. I begged Chaim to go on without me. He told me never to speak such words again. We survived together or we died together. In spite of the cold, I was sweating from the effects of the typhus, running as fast as I could, and from fear. I stopped long enough to take off some of the heavy clothes I was wearing. I shouldn't have, and I would regret it later; but I left those warm clothes lying there in the forest. My hand was slick with sweat from Chaim clinging to it as we ran.

We had to keep moving or risk being tracked by the dogs and shot, or taken back to be used at 5 o'clock roll call as an example of what is done to escapees. We ran when we could, stopped to rest only when I could go no further, walked, and then ran some more. We knew our only chance was to get as far away from Sobibor as possible before additional troops were brought in to join the search. We stumbled over trees, the bodies of those who had not made it, and each other when we were too tired to stand; but we kept moving.

The warm clothes I had left behind would be desperately needed over the next few months as we endured a bitterly cold Polish winter with few clothes and no way to build a fire or stay warm. Chaim's hand I would continue to hold for the rest of our lives together.

GERMAN DOCUMENT ON THE REVOLT
IN SOBIBOR

REPORT OF THE SECURITY POLICE IN THE LUBLIN DISTRICT — OCTOBER 15, 1943 (City of) Lublin

On October 14, 1943, at about 5:00 P.M., a revolt of Jews in the SS camp Sobibor, twenty-five miles north of Chelm. They overpowered the guards, seized the armory, and after an exchange of shots with the camp garrison, fled in unknown directions. Nine SS men murdered, one SS man missing, two foreign guards shot to death.-

Approximately 300 Jews escaped. The remainder were shot to death or are now in camp. Military police and armed forces were notified immediately and took over security of the camp at about 1:00 A.M. The area south and southwest of Sobibor is now being searched by police and armed forces.

(From the Archives of the Polish Ministry of Interior in the Jewish Historic Institute, Warsaw.)

Police report on escape from Sobibor Death Camp

CHAPTER 18

Running and Hiding

When we thought it was safe, we stopped to rest. Just as the time came for us to move on, we heard voices speaking Polish and recognized a group that had escaped from Sobibor coming through the forest. Their reaction when they saw us was immediate. They pointed to me and spoke to Chaim. I didn't understand all their words, but I understood their meaning. Chaim was welcome; I was not. Polish prisoners resented the Dutch for their former wealth, sophistication, and air of superiority and shunned them in the camp.

When Chaim refused to do what they were asking, the one with the rifle pointed it directly at his chest. Without thinking, I stepped in front of Chaim. The night became silent; no words were spoken as we stood and stared at each other. Chaim grabbed my hand, pulled me from in front of him, and we began to back away from the group. After several yards, we turned and moved quickly into the darkness of the forest. When Chaim felt we were far enough away not to be shot in the back, we turned and continued to run. We were both shaking from cold and fear, but we had survived. We were together, and we were free.

Chaim told me they had threatened to kill him if he didn't leave me behind and join them. Many times in camp, Polish people had turned their backs on Chaim because of me. They didn't like or trust anyone who was Dutch. He never complained, almost as if he were unaware that he was being shunned by his own countrymen. I know it must have been a disappointment to take harsh treatment from his own people when we were all just trying to survive the hell of Sobibor.

Many did not make it out of the camp. Some could not get through the rows of barbed wire and were left entangled for the officers with machine guns to finish off; others stepped on mines surrounding the camp. A few even felt safer not joining the escape and remained behind, only to be shot later when the Germans tried to erase any evidence of Sobibor.

I could not stop to think as we ran and prayed for darkness. Since then I have grieved for those who came so close to freedom and then did not live to claim it. Although I had nothing to do with the escape plan and never would have made it without Chaim holding my hand every step of the way, I am proud to have been part of the largest escape from any of the Nazi Camps. Without the courage and heart and planning of Sasha Pechersky and Leon Feldhendler and all who helped execute the plan, I would not be here to tell our story now.

Over three hundred prisoners tried to escape Sobibor that day. Eighty were shot or killed by the mines; one hundred more, pursued by guards, dogs, and planes, were captured and shot; and the rest ran and hid in a hostile Polish countryside. Only forty-seven survived the war, but none would have survived without the escape.

For ten nights we ran through the forest, and for ten days we looked for places to hide until darkness came again. Occasionally, but only when we had no choice, we risked getting killed or turned over to the Germans by offering people money in exchange for a hiding place. One woman refused our request for a cup of water from her well; another who fed us and let us spend the night in her cellar refused any payment. Because of or in spite of such instances, Chaim and I felt that kindness still existed in spite of all that had been done to destroy it.

I was a city girl, and every animal sound, even the wind in the trees, meant danger to me. Every tall bush looked like the greatcoat of a searching Nazi guard. Chaim educated me about the forest as he had educated me many months before about how to survive at Sobibor. Then, it was to remain invisible, steal anything that would help us survive, and stay strong by eating whatever food we could find, no matter how disgusting it was. Now, it was to stay calm, learn the sounds that were a natural part of the forest, and remind ourselves that no animal of the forest was as dangerous as the animals chasing us.

We traveled by night with Chaim using the stars to guide us. As first light became visible, we began looking for places to hide. We looked until we found some kind of shelter to protect us from the bone-numbing cold. Often we had only a thick stand of brush and trees or a haystack we could crawl in; occasionally there was a deserted farm shed far enough from the house. We were exhausted, hungry, and never warm, but I always fell asleep in his arms in the early dawn and felt safe, thankful that we had made it through one more night.

One morning a couple took some of the money Chaim had buried for our escape, and agreed to hide us for one day only. That same day German soldiers went house to house in that village, searching for escapees from Sobibor. For reasons we never knew, they skipped the one house in the village where we were hiding. The couple risked their lives by not turning us over to the SS. We didn't understand surviving such narrow escapes or the number of times we could just as easily have been caught and shot, but each close call strengthened our determination to survive.

Early one morning, two farmers stopped and asked in Polish if we wanted to pay them for a ride. Chaim answered in German and gave them a little money. They nodded at each other and agreed to take us toward the farm we were trying to reach. As their wagon moved forward, they began to speak in Polish about how when the time was right, they were going to kill us and take all our money. Chaim, of course, understood and motioned for me to get ready to slip from the back of the wagon and run into the woods. They didn't know we were gone until it was too late to catch us. If Chaim had answered them in Polish instead of German, we would not have known of their plans until it was too late. My Chaim's courage and quick thinking saved our lives yet again.

Chaim thought if we could reach a farmer he had worked for once, he might agree to hide us. We didn't get that far, but on the tenth day we found a farmer who said he would be willing to help us; but because he lived close to town, the danger of discovery was too great. Since the penalty for hiding Jews was still death for the family, and often for the whole village, we understood why he was not willing to take the risk. He did save our lives by doing what he could to help. He offered, for no pay, to take us to his brother's farm which was farther from town. With me dressed as an old woman in a long black coat and a babushka, and Chaim hiding in a hole under the hay, the farmer took us by wagon to his brother's farm near Chelm. If we had been stopped, my inability to speak Polish or one search of the hay in the back of the wagon would have been the end for all of us. We were all afraid of being discovered every mile of that trip, but no one stopped us.

When we arrived at his brother's farm, Adam, his brother, and Adam's wife Stefka thought it was too dangerous and wanted nothing to do with hiding us. They had a son to protect, and Stefka was afraid we would be discovered and the whole family killed for hiding Jews. Adam did tell Chaim we could wash at their pump before leaving. After ten days and nights of running and hiding with almost no water to drink, water to wash ourselves was a luxury.

As Chaim washed as well as he could, Stefka saw that Chaim had money hidden in bandages wrapping his legs. She motioned for Adam to follow her inside the house. When they came back out, Adam said they had agreed to let us hide in the hayloft over their cows for a short time in exchange for a share of our money. We were elated to have been given this chance we desperately needed. If we could stay in the hayloft long enough, the war might be over by the time we had to leave.

During that short time that turned into nine months, I kept a diary of our lives, and Chaim and I wrote letters to each other when we could not speak. Even now, I cannot believe that with all we had been through at Sobibor and the escape, and the ten days and nights running and hiding, that Chaim still had paper and pencil with him. As a part of telling our story, I am sharing my diary and our letters with you.

I ask you now to forgive my whining and complaining. I was very

young, spoiled, and, until the Nazis ordered us to vacate our hotel in
Zwolle, I had never experienced any hardships. Chaim never complained
and was always patient with me and my tears when I felt I could take no
more. When I read my words more than sixty years after they were written, I wonder how I could have been so spoiled, and how he could have
continued to be so patient and loving with me.

I had forgotten about my diary and the letters for many years until
Ann, who is writing these memories for me, helped me find it and asked
me to donate it to the Holocaust Museum in Washington, D.C. or the
Holocaust Museum in Israel. America was where Chaim and I had our
greatest happiness, so I sent my diary to the Holocaust Museum in Washington. You can find it there if you are interested. No matter how often I
call forth my memories or tell our story, I still do not understand. And,
unlike my Chaim, I still do not forgive.

PART FOUR

The Diary

"Sometimes love and courage are enough."

MARTIN NIEMÖLLER,
1892-1984

"First they came for the Socialists, and I did not
speak out Because I was not a Socialist.
Then they came for the Trade Unionists,
and I did not speak out
Because I was not a Trade Unionist.
Then they came for the Jews, and I did not
speak out Because I was not a Jew.
Then they came for me —
and there was no one left to speak for me."

SPEECH FOR THE CONFESSING CHURCH, 1946

The Loft

Our home for nine months, from October 24, 1943, to July 26, 1944, was a tiny hay loft in Adam and Stefka Nowak's barn near Chelm, Poland. We had room to stand only in the center of the loft, so we had to spend most of our time sitting or lying down on the hay. Our loft was dark except for one hole in the corner of the roof, which let in a little light on bright days, but it also let in the rain, and cold, and snow. During the night or on dark days, and there were many that winter, there was not enough light to write. It was a bitterly cold Polish winter, and I wished many times for the heavy coat I had left in the forest after the escape. When warm weather finally came, we had the flies, and heat, and smells from the animals below, from our toilet pail in the corner, and from each other. We often had no water to drink, and washing was a luxury we didn't even think about. There was never enough food because the Nowaks had so little even for themselves. If anybody came to visit them, we got nothing because there wasn't enough for everybody. But we survived.

We were young and in love, and we were, for the time being, free. In spite of the suffering and the harsh conditions you will read about in my diary, we were thankful, and happy, and full of hope ... most of the time. Or that's how I remember it now.

Saartje's Diary with Chaim and Saartje's Letters

Poland October 24, 1943

(1)

Suddenly a feeling came over me to write down everything we experienced, my husband and I, in Poland. First of all, I am going to tell you where I am with my dearly beloved husband. We are on a farm, above the horses, in the hay and there is a small window through which the light enters during the day, just barely enough to see each other. Despite these difficult circumstances we are still thankful and happy that we are alive after having escaped from Sobibor.

(2)

This is a diary in which I want to write you how happy I am. My dearest friend who is everything to me, is sitting next to me. We are in a hayloft and we live together in a corner, a sheet flat on the straw that is under us, and at night we cover ourselves with straw, not with hay. My Chaim and I have been here for 16 days now. I never thought that it would be so wonderful to be married.

(3)

First of all what I still remember most is the escape from Sobibor. There was talk for at least a week under great secrecy that something was going to happen, there was no work in the camp and we thought, what appeared to be true in retrospect, that we would otherwise not have lived another 14 days. My dearest Chaim knew everything of course, but he was not allowed to tell me anything.

(4)

At 3 o'clock, Chaim came to me and told me, "Make sure you are at the warehouse at 3:30". I was there on time. Five minutes later Porzyczki, a Kapo, arrived and ten minutes later he killed Wulf at camp III. After that, five men went to Beckman, including my beloved husband, and they also stabbed him. It was retaliation for the 10,000 Jews he had killed. I quickly went to see where my Chaim was and he came to me with two deep wounds (which I am quite worried about right now, since I am not able to take very good care of them).

(5)

I think back to when I arrived at Sobibor.

(6)

We arrived at that camp at two in the afternoon. Lots of German soldiers yelling with mean faces and sticks in their hands. An old woman walks in front of me. They hit her. Suddenly we are told to discard our bags. Thus we throw aside our backpacks. After walking a little further we see two Nazi soldiers standing and they ask us, "Are you married?" We say "No," so they tell us to go and stand over to one side. So we stood there, some twenty girls separated out of a transport of 3000 people.

(7)

We arrive at a small barrack where they asked our names and they told us where we had to sleep. In the afternoon we went to work. We had to sort the contents of the backpacks of the people. We did not know what was going on in Sobibor. We thought, such good food from the people's bags and clothing, anything you could ever want, chocolate, cigarettes, the most beautiful clothes. Until that night I spoke with Maurits Zukerndelaar and

(8)

with Man Troostwijk from Zwolle, who told me that all of the people with whom I had come and all of those that had come before were gassed and cremated. They showed me a large fire in Camp III where 10,000 had already been cremated. Impossible to believe, but it is true.

(9)

When you arrive, the women go to the right and the men to the left and they tell you that you are going to take a bath. Thus, first the women who already walked to the bath house and stripped down naked in a barrack for that purpose and go to the next barrack (there are 3 barracks, the last is the bath house) where some 30 young Jewish men, which are boys from our camp have to work. We sleep in camp I, we work in camp II, and in camp III we are murdered, but nobody from

(10)

the first two camps goes in there. Or, if they do get in, they don't come out of camp III again. Well, these 30 men who stand there, they cut off all the hair of the women. My husband, who I came to know in the camp, always had to go along or be shot. It is a horrible, horrible thing to have to do; he will never be able to forget. To see so many young people walk to their deaths. Chaim tells me that the Dutch women really do not know what is happening to them and many cried because their hair was being cut off.

(11)

Thank God that they did not know what was going to happen to them on these Polish transports to a much greater enemy. One by one these people know that they are heading for death. Children, 4 and 5 years old, they know it. It is terrible to see how these women and children were hit by these moffen (a Dutch pejorative word for German). They have leather whips with which they hit. I have personally felt this myself on more than one occasion, especially from the men. I can still see it before my eyes. Everything happens

(12)

very fast and the people who are arriving and they throw aside the bags they have with them. And if they do not, they get hit. Many women carry their children in their arms and they also have a lot of bags with them. A woman quickly throws her backpack away, but her child is taken from her. She calls out, "Oh, God, my child, my child," and she wants to go back to get her child. A German soldier sees her and tells her to keep on walking and he hits the woman in the

(13)

face, so that the blood streams down her face and still she yells out, "My child," and she is hit again and she yells, "my child". The German soldier tells her, "We will take care of your child." After that we sorted the bags and many times we found a child among them. I cannot write everything that I experienced and I just hope that some people will survive these camps to tell the story. This is a disgrace for every German, because they all wanted their Hitler.

(14)

I continue about the women. Thus, they lost their hair and they come into the barrack with all the showers, where gas comes out, instead of water.

(15)

I don't know why we lived and others did not. We fought for the right to live and we were successful because we got out of that terrible place. Others fought just as hard but could not make it. Chaim and I love each other so much and wanted so much to live like all other people. We have already lost all our family. God help us out of this misery. We have seen thousands of people walking to their deaths and we are bringing a new person into the world for us to walk to our deaths in this way. Why were we not gassed as Jews at Sobibor so we do not have to experience this misery? Although now I have my beloved man and I am completely happy with him.

* * * * *

Letter to Chaim

My eternal love,

I have much happiness in my life. To have such a good man gives me a purpose for living. I don't know much German; therefore, I finish this with many kisses.
From Your Selma.

* * * * *

(16)

I woke up and heard the birds sing so beautifully that for a moment I thought I was in Zwolle, until I saw reality and had to think about where we are. We are hiding in a hayloft, and I now know we are expecting a child. My mother never told me anything, and Stefka thought I was pregnant before I knew. I noticed that some liquid was coming from my breasts. I know I must be pregnant. This is terrible. What should we do now. This is going to cost us our lives. By these people where we are hidden, we cannot have a child. We are lying here for three days, crying. We do not know what to do. If we go outside we will be shot to death. We also cannot go to a doctor because they do not help Jews. We have thought about everything, but we don't know what to do. We just have to wait and see.

Chaim's Letter to Selma

> *To my dearest wife,*
> *Your latest news, that you are pregnant has made me extremely happy. Unbelievable! Yes, Yes, stupid, it is known to be very stupid to do something like this. But, my dear wife, it has happened and we cannot do anything about it. Let's not be broken by what will happen in half a year from now. We have also a lot of chance that everything will turn out well. There is one thing I know, that I love you very much, as much as is possible. We have to live day by day and patiently wait what time will bring us.*
> *Thousand kisses, my beloved Selma,*
> *Your husband Chaim*

                         * * * * *

(17)

Hopefully the Russians will come over here and we can be treated like human beings. Yesterday was a very bad day. We were really in the dumps because of my condition because we could not stay in our hiding place with a baby. Stefka came and said she wanted the ring, which represents the last of our money. She was afraid that we did not want to give it to her. She had

(18)

already received 7000 guilders from us in gold. She is so mean. Not that we are attached to money, but we may still have to run because of the baby. God help us that we do not have to run again and look for a roof over our heads. Thus, we now have no more money and we are in a country that looks at us with much hatred. We have no way to pay for a hiding place. A feeling to be on earth should be beautiful, but now that is not possible for us. Oh, to try not to think about tomorrow. This minute we are still happy and we don't think beyond that.

* * * * *

Chaim's Birthday Letter to Selma

> *May 3, 1944*

> *Dear Selma,*
> *We are now in the nicest month of the year, the month of May. Everything begins to live again. And will we? We have to be up here in the loft and wait. We wait for a new life. And I believe so strongly that it will come.*

> *We have to be patient and persevere. Everyday that we have survived will bring us closer to our goal. May has very special meaning for me. Very soon you will have your birthday on the 15th of May.*

> *Unfortunately, I cannot give you anything for your birthday. Hopefully, once we are free your birthdays will be very different.*

Be healthy and don't overdo it.
A thousand kisses and another kiss.
Your husband who loves you very much,
Chaim

* * * * *

(19)

It is Monday morning and I woke up with a very good feeling. Today I became 22 years old and this is the first year that I am so intimate together with my Chaim and that we are married. The day began with a wonderful wish expressed by my darling that next year we would be together in The Netherlands. That face of my husband, expressing such a nice wish, that was the most beautiful gift

(20)

he could have given to me. A little while later, Adam came and brought us a bouquet of flowers, which was such a tremendous surprise, to receive something so beautiful and I also received flowers from Stefka with the most beautiful and best wishes that we would soon be free and that we would not forget Adam and Stefka. A pity that my family is not alive to know that I am married to such a good husband.

(21)

This is already my second birthday in Poland; the first was in Sobibor. At that time I knew my husband perhaps two weeks and we were not as intimate as we are now and my birthday was not as nice, having to sort through the bags of hundreds of Jews who had been murdered. Even if we had eaten salmon, chocolates, real butter and black bread, the potatoes we had this morning tasted 100 times better than anything could have tasted in Sobibor.

(22)

We now live with the one hope that the war will come to an end and that we will experience freedom again like all other people. And that the wishes of my husband and of Stefka and Adam may not be far away. Amen. Oh, we will always remember the two people who hid us. Oh, may we live to see that and repay them. Oh, God, let us live!!

(23)

May 18, 1944

Early this morning, Adam came and said that we would have to stay above the pig barn for a couple of days. Why? Yesterday, Adam's sister-in-law was below our stable and we did not hear anything and Chaim walked around and the boards went up and down and we betrayed us. What to do now? Then the woman went outside and yelled out, with the whole family standing around. This is enough to drive you crazy, all the things we have to go through.

(24)

Adam told her it was a cresant (unknown meaning) who was staying with them, thus the sister-in-law knows that a month ago she also had that at her own house. Thus, this morning we had to leave the little sunlight we had. We are now in a nearly dark attic, where I almost cannot see anything, including my writing. While I am writing this, a cuckoo is flying around our stable and is constantly calling out. I hope it brings luck, since we have enough misfortune already.

(25)

When I had to walk from one stable to the other, I was not able to put weight on my toes. I forgot how to walk and I almost fell over. What else will happen to us? Will this be the end? Do we have to endure even more? I am at my end; this is altogether too much for me.

Pages with a sketch of a building and floor plan, and a couple of sketches of dresses. {these sketches are included in the United States Holocaust Museum in Washintgon, D.C.]

Hotel Wijnberg
Zwolle
Holland

Selma Engel Wijnberg
Chaim Engel

Chaim and Selma Engel

Selma Wijnberg
Veemarktstraat 23
Zwolle
Telephone 4101

At home somewhere on a farm in Poland

(26)

In October,1942, my Mother and the boys went to Poland and were killed. Hopefully, Bram and Jettie and their 2 children are still alive in Holland. In addition, Bep also went to Poland and the rest of my dear aunts and uncles.

(27)

This notebook serves the purpose of recalling my memories of the time I spent with my husband hidden in a hayloft somewhere in Poland. And the hope to one day live like a free person again.

(28)

In Poland, June 21, 1944

It is not my desire to only write about the misery and grief, but also about the happiness.

(29)

Everything takes a lot of time here, especially when it concerns spending money. Stefka traveled before to Chelm, but she did not bring any ointment. This disease won't kill you she said, and we had sleepless nights for 3 weeks because we were scratching ourselves all night long. And it got worse each day and nothing was done about it. I was and am looking miserable and it is becoming totally unbearable. Besides, I could be 6 weeks pregnant, and being aware of this, maybe something can be done about it. We are staying with honest people. He is a good man but he is henpecked.

(30)

Stefka is a woman as hard as a rock and has no compassion. Thus she was complaining that there was no money in the house. What to do? Stefka was going to go to Chelm to make some money, but we knew already that she would come back without bringing anything for us. And thus my husband and I took the fountain pen from our last bit of capital and we told them that they had to buy ointment and medicine with that. Everything was fine and Adam was going to go to Chelm, but Adam went along with Stefka.

(31)

We knew that they would come back with one small jar of ointment. And, yes Mrs. came back with two little jars of ointment, which wasn't much, and nothing else. They supposedly couldn't get enough for the fountain pen. What to do now? We talked about it all day and we didn't know what to do. Until in the evening Chaim said, "Selma, you know what we do, we give them the watch as well and then they will do it. Better to be without a cent than not to be healthy."

(32)

In the evening Adam came and Chaim told him that we would also give them the watch and that he was therefore to go to Chelm to the doctor, I am writing this now in a much lighter mood than it really was. What this really cost us in health is indescribable but you could read it from our faces. Thus, on Saturday, June 17, 1944, Adam went to Chelm in order to buy medicine, ointment and other things we needed, because during the 8 months we have now been here we have denied ourselves everything that would cost a red cent. We don't even ask for a match, and there are many things we need. We ask for nothing.

(33)

How often has it happened that we had no water upstairs to have a sip to drink and then we just think, if only we will survive this war, then everything will be fine and we are willing to make any sacrifice for that. Coming back to the story about Adam, we thought that everything would now finally be resolved. He went to the doctor. In the evening he returned from Chelm and jokingly told us, and we didn't know it was a joke, that he had not bought anything. And I said, "Oh, why did you not at least buy us a little gift?" But thank God he had ointment, 5 boxes, iron for my anemia and

(34)

some other little things. The last thing he said is that the watch did not bring much. It was worth 200 zlotys, but he did not get that and that is the main reason he did not go to the doctor and buy anything for when I get my period. And so, there is a big chance I am pregnant. But it is still a joy that we are now a week further and the itching is almost gone. My husband is completely free of itching, whereas I still have some left and my wounds are not completely healed. Nevertheless, I am starting to feel like a human being again and my husband also. But I am always running a fever and a white effluence that makes me feel weak. I am now taking iron and I hope that this will help. There is always something.

(35)

Today Chaim had such a toothache and we washed all the ointment off. But I cannot be really happy as my sweetheart is in so much pain.

(36)

Chaim told Adam that I need more food because I am getting weaker. Adam said that was good. But it still has to come from the woman. The day before she did not want to give us anything. Then she got the watch and brought us some food. She did not even ask how I was doing. But everything is fine. My husband had two pairs of socks when we came here. Of those, we left one pair with them to be washed. And since we don't go out on the street and we can't go for walks, they just kept the socks for themselves. But the worst is that Chaim's socks are completely worn. Thus, I unraveled the socks

(37)

and knitted a new pair from the wool. When I did not have my period in two months she could see in my eyes that I was pregnant and when liquid began flowing from my breasts I was sure that it was so. She caused me grief by saying she knew I was pregnant and that it happens quite often with young women. I have done a lot of sewing and knitting for her, but I never got any word of gratitude from her. My coat is my entire possession. We put everything into the oven to kill the itching that causes us so much trouble. Chaim asked whether the clothes could support the heat of the oven. And she said, "No problem." He asked her twice

(38)

and she said that everything could go into the oven. Until yesterday, when the clothes came back upstairs, we discovered that my coat was burned and destroyed. At first I was very angry, until Chaim said, "don't cry, we have already lost so much, our whole family, and if we now lose our own lives that would be worse."

(39)

June 22

Thank God, the night is over. Chaim did not sleep the whole night because of his toothache, and I myself could not sleep because of the itching. The itch eats you. Breakfast is over and we wait again for lunch, just like every other day. Fortunately, I have work to do today. I am knitting a pullover for Adam. My husband is also happy because he can help me to wind the yarn into a ball. So he has something to do for half an hour. This is our life. We sit in our shirts on a blanket and keep ourselves covered with an old sack. And like this one day passes after another. Today is the first day of summer. We would prefer it to be winter because we live above a stable, and not only our toilet bucket is under our noses. That's the way it is when it becomes a little warmer, there is an unpleasant odor everywhere.

(40)

And we are going through all this just to wait and hope and pray for our freedom. Is it worthwhile to suffer so much? And yet we are happy, my Chaim and I, and we therefore are patiently waiting, with the hope that together we will still have a good life. Amen. It is 7 o'clock in the evening. I have been knitting all day long. I don't know what's wrong with me, but I am dead tired. My legs are like lead. Where is this going? To be so weak is terrible.

(41)

All day long, liquid is coming out of my breasts. Too bad that my mother did not tell me anything. I knew nothing, absolutely nothing, and we are paying for that right now. It is almost 8 o'clock and the cows are being driven into the stable. This means for us to lie as quietly as mummies for half an hour. My sweetheart is now sleeping since he did not sleep last night and he is worrying about me very much. Oh, he is such a good man and so sweet with me.

(42)

We hope to gain our freedom. I am always writing the same thing, but I can't help it. We long so desperately for freedom. But now it is getting dark and we are waiting for the evening bread. Then we go to sleep and hope that we will wake up healthy.

(43)

June 24

Yesterday I did not feel like writing; many days I don't. Chaim did not feel well. He had terrible abdominal cramps and he felt miserable. Yesterday they butchered a pig and a calf. And we had thought about that all week that it would be so nice when we got a piece of meat. Until now we have only had some broth with two bones and other than that we have not seen anything. But everything is fine as long as we survive this war. Today Adam went to Chelm in order to sell half of the calf. We are waiting eagerly for his return as a lot depends on that for us. Today went very fast as I was knitting the sleeve of the pullover.

(44)

It was raining the whole day, and I have such a longing to sit with my mother and to talk to her again and the boys and to look at their faces. I also believe that one of these days, Leo, the son of Bram, is having a birthday. Oh, if you are still living, Bram, Jettie, and the children, then we still have family. Very often Chaim and I say, "If Bram is still alive." Everything is taking so long, it is almost two years since I left home and 18 months that my family is no longer living. They died so young. I still see it before me. Maurits and Bep with us in the Voorstraat. How happy they were!

(45)

They were married for 4 weeks. But of one thing I am convinced, they did not know that they went to their deaths. Incidentally, today I thought about the women in Sobibor whose husbands were a little sick and went to lie down. When the women came back from work at 12 o'clock, totally exhausted, and they wanted to quickly eat a bite together with their husbands, because they too were hungry. Everything had to be done very quickly because the noon break was only an hour. So they come to the beds and see no man. Where is my husband? But they did not have to look very far.

(46)

That morning a "cleaning action" had taken place among the sick men. Thus, all of them had been shot to death. Yes, it is a strange comfort that our family did not have to go through this. I forgot to mention that my Chaim is again feeling 100% well as far as his health is concerned. This husband of mine slept half a day. But the bad thing is that he has nothing to do. Now we are waiting for Adam and hoping that he may come home healthy and well. It is already 8:30 pm and we are watching for more than an hour, but still no sign of Adam. I am already so nervous, until Chaim sees him coming. Thank God, this worry is behind us. I am writing this in the dark.

(47)

Monday, July 3, 1944, Poland

Today I want to write something. Time is going fast. It is already 14 days ago since I last wrote. There is not much news that would give us hope that the end of this war is nearing. I cannot write much, because for us every day is the same. For the last few days I have been feeling much better and am not running a fever. We are not rid of the itching yet. This week, if everything goes well, and if Adam comes back healthy, he will go to Chelm to buy some more ointment and go to the doctor for me. Yesterday Adam went to his

(48)

brother to buy two pigs. He is not back yet. I hope that he will be back soon. My knitting worked out well and I knitted for Edek a pullover and a pair of pants which for us is a good fortune as our relationship has improved. Another miracle is that I am going to make a skirt for Stefka and that she even gave me yarn for a skirt for myself. I have no skirt; I have only a pair of long pants. This is the latest news in our lives. Chaim has a growth on his finger, which causes him great pain. The weather is beautiful and I yearn to go for a walk outside. But this is not possible.

(49)

It is already more than eight months since I have been with people other than my husband. Although this gives me great joy, sometimes

I cannot suppress this desire to be with other people, especially my family. Also I don't know why in the last months I had no sexual desire. Maybe I am frigid, but I do love my husband very much. Hopefully, this is caused by the type of life that we are living here. I am sitting the entire day in my undershirt and without knitting and writing there is nothing to do. We now have again to sleep.

(50)

Their whole family came to visit and the brother-in-law is walking around the place. In the afternoon, we were lying for half an hour dead quiet and not moving. We did speak when we did not know he was near and now we have to wait and see if he heard us. Now we are sitting like we are dead. There is always something.

(51)

Fortunately, he did not hear us. We were fortunate because otherwise we would have had to leave this place. Hopefully, nothing more will happen so that we will not give ourselves away. Adam came back today. Apart from him, nobody was here.

(52)

Sabbath, July 8, 1944

Today is so warm that you perspire even if you sit quietly. And we are here above the stable and the flies are eating us. Sometimes it is unbearable. But one good thing we heard today, that the moffen (Germans) are retreating on all fronts. Oh actually, we should be joyful

(53)

that it goes so well on all fronts. However, it is hard for us to find any joy because of what happened in this war, and we are without any family. For us Jews this war is already lost because of what we lost. Changing the subject, Adam was supposed to go to Chelm to buy ointment. But he still has to go. There is always something happening when something has to be done for us. He now tells that they are arresting people at work. But because of this we are here without ointment and my hands and feet are blistering again from the eczema. Yes, we gave

(54)

a watch as extra payment, and in spite of that we cannot get anything done in return. Now Adam says that he will go, but Stefka says that he won't go. Now we just have to wait and see what will happen. If he does not go, we'll have to have a serious talk with them. Whenever our money had to be spent on us we always get into an argument. And I don't know what I have, I am so nervous. We cannot sit still because the flies are stinging too much and I am too dirty to look at. I am already wearing a shirt of Chaim's for three weeks and it smells, etc. etc. That is our life and there is not much joy and

(55)

days go by without there being a smile on our faces and my feet are worse and worse.

(56)

July 10, 1944
Still nobody has gone to Chelm for ointment and things are starting to look bad for us again. Now Stefka says that she will go to Chelm tomorrow, but she does not want to buy more than two jars which is nothing. We cannot stand it here anymore because of the flies and the heat. All day long we are waving a handkerchief through the air to chase away the flies. And now we are suffering

(57)

from ulcers and itching. Oh, life does not have such a great value
for us any longer to go through all this suffering. Thus, this evening we will go downstairs and then it will be make or break. We
cannot go on like this any longer, to be mistreated like this. Everything is fine, but when your health, your life are at stake, there
are limits to what one can accept. So for us it is better to be dead
and that will be decided. We will still have some human dignity.

(58)

July 13, 1944

We did not go downstairs on Monday and on Tuesday Stefka
went to Chelm and she came back with two jars of ointment, the
worst quality she could get. What shall we do? For one day we
were not very friendly, but that did not help. Then Chaim spoke
with Adam yesterday and reminded him of all the values in gold
and diamonds we had given them so that they could buy things
for us and we gave them an extra watch and still we do not get
the medicine we so desperately need. Now it seems that Adam did
not transmit the message properly so this morning Stefka comes
steaming in anger, blaming us that we regret to have given them
so much money.

(59)

And she let us feel that we are Jews and they can give us the ring
back and that we should leave and try to stay with other people.
This she tells us about every week. So there is always something and
all one can do is grin and bear it in order to get a smile in return.
Now Chaim still has to talk to the witch. Even if she does a lot for
us, she is a real witch and always turns our words around. Chaim
always says from a wicked person you cannot expect anything good.
And that is the truth. One thing we know, if God allows us to live,
we will live.

(60)

It is good to be good to yourself and for somebody else not to is hard. We really should go down and talk to them. But it is the 13th and we don't know yet what to do.

(61)

Sabbath, July 15, 1944
Today I woke up in a good mood. Thank God, we are again good friends with Stefka. She talked to Chaim and everything is okay. She said that she had no money and thus she could not buy things. We agreed with everything, since for now we have ointment and we shall see what happens later on. But we always are the inferior ones because we still are Jews. Adam is a weakling and he has nothing to say. She said

(62)

to Chaim that she does not let him go. My Chaim wants so badly to go to America! Otherwise there is not much news. I am knitting a pullover for Stefka. Chaim is knitting a pair of socks and it is raining. This morning we ate noodles and further we are in good health. Chaim is losing his thumbnail but it does not hurt. May God grant that we have a good day and that Adam's brother will come home healthy and well. Yesterday we both had 8 cherries. The first ones we ate in the morning and the last ones on Sabbath afternoon. Yet there is some news to tell about us. We were able to take a complete bath and for the first time this year we received a fresh sheet and

(63)

a cover for our feather blanket and we are also clean ourselves. I hope that we succeeded in washing away the skin rash and that I am not pregnant. There is no further news. It is 4 o'clock and we go to have a nap.

July 16
Adam came back with pigs and a stranger, thus half a ration for lunch. The pullover is finished.

Monday, July 17
Rain is better than heat. We are healthy and slept until 10 am Otherwise, a strong desire for freedom. I spoke with my husband about the family.

July 18
Adam came home drunk this morning. He can't handle the drink. I am longing to be with other people in a normal situation. It is a gloomy day and this causes the mood to be sad.

(64)

We have not been outside during the day for 9 months. Since 14 days we hear that the front is approaching. We hope that they will soon be here. There is a great chance that Chaim would then have to join the army. In that case I would be going too, although I don't have any papers as they were burned in Sobibor. Now we wait and see what today will bring. We heard bombing quite near us during the night. I am going to knit a pullover for Adam. Thank God, I have again some work to do. Chaim is still busy knitting his socks with yarn we gather from different remnants from what I knit for Stefka.

July 19, 1944
One does not know what the day will bring, and what I wrote yesterday still holds true today. We have been discovered. Last night, the 18th, Tatjoe, the son of the brother-in-law, climbed up the stairs to catch a young bird.

(65)

Instead he caught us for good. He had seen us when we came 9 months ago and so he certainly recognized us. He said to Stefka, "Are those the same people and where have they been?" Now what we have always feared has happened. What should we do now? Of course, he told everything at home and if they get to know that we are Jews we will have to leave. Oh, God, why did this have to happen now? Just yesterday we were saying, "If we survive this war it will be a great miracle." Will this now be our end? Can there ever be a period of time when nothing happens? We don't know yet, because it happened late last night, and we will we have to do something today. Will we have to leave? Will we have to walk again at night without knowing

(66)

whether we can stay alive or if we will have a roof over our heads. Now we are waiting, so much good we cannot expect from this day. It is 4 o'clock in the morning. We are far away. I mean, we can hear the front. There is still some hope and it seems that the situation may change. One may have only hope in this life, and that is all we have. It is 8 am and we don't know anything, and a stranger is in the house. We don't know what is happening and we are waiting impatiently. God help us! So many people have cried this out before. It is raining. What if we have to walk without adequate clothes to cover us? It is 10 am and Stefka brought our breakfast. She told us that Tatjoe did recognize us and that he has told everything at home. They have already been asked if they received a lot of money from us. Now we wait and see what will happen. It will not be very good. Today the front

(67)

can be heard very well. It is 3 o'clock in the afternoon. Maybe this time things have turned out well after all. Adam told Tatjoe that we were evacuated here only a few weeks ago and that we will soon be leaving. If they now keep their mouths shut everything will be all right. Only his mother and grandmother know about it. His father does not know anything, and this is good because he is a drinker. Hopefully, liberation will come soon. And the brother-in-law knows.

July 20

Today no news. We feel relieved as long as nothing happens. The pullover for Adam is cancelled. It is going to be a skirt for Stefka. The front can be heard very clearly. As I am putting away this note-book Adam shows up and tells that his brother came by and left his horse and his household goods here because the fighting was so close to his farm. That means that the front is about 40 km from here.

(68)

And where his brother lives there are many wounded German soldiers. And this is 12 km from the front. A German said that it is such a large offensive that they are not able to hold their position. On Tuesday, we heard shooting for the first time. Tatjoe came upstairs and talked to Chaim. He is a nice boy. Stefka gave us so little to eat at lunchtime that since 4 pm my stomach is aching from hunger.

Friday, July 21

During the entire night we could clearly hear the front. This morn-ing we heard nothing yet except for many Russian airplanes in the air. We are healthy, but the flies are eating us up and once again

I am in a bad mood. To attempt to stay in such a miserable place

(69)

and I don't understand the people. To be so far away from Holland makes me so sad and I cannot hold back my tears.

2 o'clock in the afternoon
In the afternoon, while I am writing this I see a lot of military vehicles coming in, some 50, so things are starting to move here too. Also, Adam's brother came. He left his farm when it went up in flames. They are getting the potatoes out of the field. Right now there is a lot of bombing all around us. What will this day bring us? It is about 8 pm and the night is approaching. More people are coming because they had to leave their farms. Today we did not hear anything from the front. It is 9 pm and still there are cars passing by.

July 22
The war is advancing well, so they say. The Germans are leaving and we see many cars. They say that Chelm

(70)

has already been freed. And I have to write down something remarkable, how people can meet. When we walked from Sobibor we came early in the morning by Polish people, and they gave us milk and bread without asking us to pay for it. We asked them about the way and they told us that they did not know the area. So they directed us toward to Adam's brother and there we went, and from that brother's place we were brought here. Now all the people are gone from that farm and all the people who helped us are now at Adam's farm. People are meeting each other, but [illegible].

(71)

Adam brought us a cigarette, a German was here, and he got the cigarette from that German. He did not realize that in the end a Jew would smoke his cigarette. This morning a mof wanted a horse from Adam. So Adam ran away very fast and the German yelled at him to stop, but Adam continued to run. The moffen are now here in the village. Thus they are still in Chelm as well. So we have to wait and trust that things will go well.

4 o'clock in the afternoon
Even before 12 o'clock there were never so many moffen in the village as today. Now we are more afraid than ever before.

Sunday, July 23
Since 3 days we have heard nothing from the front. It appears that the moffen are walking away without shooting. The front has already passed us in Krasnystaw, 28 km from here. We hear bombardments, but there are

(72)

moffen in the villages around us. We are still not seeing any Russians, so we continue in hiding. It is not yet 12 0'clock. It is difficult to bring food to us because the whole family is here plus the strangers. Last night she gave us a piece of bread and we will have to make do with that. Where there is a will there is a way, but now it is hard to find a will. Our goal is to survive the war even if it we're on nothing more than bread and water. We still don't know anything new and just have to wait what the day has in store for us.

It is now 8 in the morning.

It is now 7 in the evening and I don't know anything new. The moffen are leaving and we see them going fast by car. They don't know where to go because they are circled in by the Russians. We do hear a lot of shooting from all around us and bombardments

(73)

especially in the west. This means that the Russians are already well past us. We are still hiding here upstairs. It seems that my belly is growing, I know I am pregnant. Also I am beginning to see spots all over my body again and the itching is coming back. It is now almost dark and cars are still moving. May God grant that we will wake up tomorrow in good health and without the moffen.

Monday, July 24
We did not hear much shooting during the night. The whole night we heard vehicles moving. Thus they are fleeing fast. These could be military vehicles or they could be [illegible]. There is shooting out in the west. At about 9 o'clock in the morning Adam came and told us that the Russians are now 5 km from us. So there is a big chance for the front to come here. The front may come to Chelm

(74)

where the Russians already are. The Russians have not arrived in Krasnystaw yet. Adam told his brother and sister-in-law that we are here since 9 months and we are still here because the clock has not yet struck 12 o'clock. It is now 2 pm and Chaim is downstairs in order to tell that the Soviets are coming. We are seeing a lot of military. Has the moment come where we will be considered human beings again? It is incredible! I am sitting outside on the pasture together with my Chaim. We are free!! The Soviets are here and so we can walk outside. Why don't I feel more joy? I don't know. In front of us we see the first Soviet patrols passing by. May God grant that everything will go well. The front is right now

(75)

4 km away from us. Chaim and I are lying in the wheat field. [illegible] It is around 9 o'clock and the front is still 4 km in front of us. I hope they don't retreat, otherwise we could be lost at the last moment. God, help us, we are so eager to live! Maybe it would have been better if we would have moved further away from the front. We just don't know. You have to be lucky and hopefully we will be fortunate. I am sitting in the wheat field while I am writing this and Chaim went to some people to find out what is happening. May God help us.

July 25
I still can't believe it and the Russians are about 20 km from here and they are heading forward, they say.

Wednesday, July 26
Yesterday I did not write any more. Chaim did not like it that I

(76)

was writing outside, but today I am allowed to do it. It is unbelievable! We really are free and I am really writing outside!! Is it true? We continuously have to tell ourselves that it is really true. We are human beings again and we can talk to other people! Chaim talked this morning with two Russians and he thanked them for giving us our freedom back. We went to the village, 1 km walking, to see a doctor because of my pregnancy. I am pregnant for sure. My belly is growing. What else could it be? Not that he would have diagnosed something. He was a student and there was nothing he could do for me. We also went to Adam's brother-in-law. It causes me pain to visit

(77)

families and to realize that we have lost everything and I cannot help it that it causes me much pain to meet other people. As soon as it appears that the front is no longer in Chelm we will go there to try to obtain new documents for me. On the way back from the village I could not walk anymore. My legs felt like lead. May God help us that we can go back to Holland strong and healthy and that Bram might still be alive, and that we may still have some good friends there who will kindly receive us and who will help us. I am always afraid that there is no kindness left in this world. Since we have been living downstairs we have not found any kindness yet.

(78)

Do I feel rejected because I do not understand the people? I hope this is the reason!! Chaim is helping Adam with the peat and I am knitting.

Sabbath, July 29
We have been walking for a couple of days and we are working. Yesterday I did the laundry and for the first time it was clean. That I am pregnant is great news for us. Probably I am already in the 6th month. My belly is growing by the day. I hope the child can be born in Holland and that it will be healthy. Then we should be able to accept the message of freedom with joy, in spite of the fact that it would have been better if

(79)

the baby would have come a bit later. Chaim is helping in the field where they are binding the rye. Tomorrow we are going to Chelm if all goes well. There is always some money problem. Now they don't want to give us anything back on the ring. Well, the main thing is that God does not leave us and that good fortune will stay with us. We still have two good hands with which we can earn our daily bread. I still cannot walk very well and my feet are swollen and hurting. Since we are living downstairs we have not received a friendly word from Stefka yet.

Sunday, July 30
It is unbelievable; we are right now in Chelm together with about 100 Jews. Even Jews from Sobibor!

(80)

Koert and Ulla and another Sobibor inmate are alive. It is unbelievable! Adam took us along to Chelm. We already had a house where we could sleep, and we thought that we should go to Flodawa, but we stayed here in Chelm together with the other Jews. Oh, God, help us to find a roof over our heads and that I may keep my dear husband with me. What will this day bring us? There are many Russian soldiers here, as well as Jews. It will be as it will be and everything will turn out for good.

(81)

Monday, July 31
Right now it is maybe 5 o'clock and I am writing this in a nice room with 4 beds. We sleep here together with 3 other men. This is actually a house where a mof used to live, and now they are putting Jews in it. Nobody is helping us and many of these people don't even have clothes. My God, did they fight for this, to live as

outcasts? What will this day bring us? Koert went to Moscow. If Chaim would have asked for money and if he had received it we would now be rich, 200 Zlotys. I hope that Chaim does not have to join the army. I don't think that I would get through by myself if my sweetheart would not be with me anymore. Where will this lead to?

(82)

Sunday, August 6

We have already been in Chelm for a week and we did some sowing work in order to earn some money. We also went to the doctor and I am very weak. I cannot walk and my feet are swollen and hurting. Also my belly is very big and my pants are too tight and do not fit anymore. Actually, I cannot wear these pants anymore. Chaim got to know a captain at the hospital and he will be admitted to work at the hospital. We hope that this will help that Chaim does not have to leave me. We are now living in a house with other Jews and we sleep in a bed.

(83)

We lie on the bed and cover ourselves with our clothes. We are very poor and I don't know where all this will lead us. My feet hurt me even when I sit. We have no money to go to a good doctor. We don't sleep well because there is always somebody who wakes us up. Is this our freedom? Is this what we looked forward to? Oh God, help us. We cannot go on like this much longer.

Monday, August 7
[illegible]

Sunday, August 13
We are now 2 weeks in Chelm and Chaim is working with the

Red Cross. I am sitting in the house the whole day together with
other Jews in one room full

(84)

of hay for the cows. Life is very difficult and very hard to bear...
[illegible] My leg is [illegible]. It is a large wound and I have a lot
of pain. Is this the freedom we longed for so long? Does this have
to go on like this? Oh, God, I can't take any more. I don't have the
strength [illegible] I don't do anything but cry.

(85)

It probably will not be a happy child and Chaim has to work and
I am always sad. Why does it have to be like this?

* * * * *

Selma's Letter to Chaim

> *My Dearest Husband,*
> *My wish is that you will always be with me. God grant that you*
> *will stay healthy and we will be in Holland very quickly with*
> *Bram and Jettie and the kids. Oh, we would be so happy!!*
> *Your Selma*

* * * * *

Friday, August 24
We are [illegible] and we do not have a roof over our heads yet and
we are going from one corner to another and we get [several lines
illegible]. I can't go on like this. I would like to have some water,
but it seems that is not allowed. God let me die.

(86)

[illegible page]

Our Hope

[German to English dictionary]

das fernrohr	telescope
versuchen	to try
die vernunft	reason
wahlen	to choose
entfernen	to remove
das innere	inside
unterlassen	to omit, to abstain from
unweit	not far from
mittels	with
kraft	strength
wahrend	while
vermoge	by virtue of
ungeachtet	regardless of
oberhalb	above
unterhalb	below
laut	noisy
halber	half
wegen	because of
untern	those below
statt	instead
um	about (and other meanings according to context)
langs	along, alongside

To try not to think about tomorrow. This minute we are still happy and we don't think beyond that.

My diary ends with those words, but my memories of those times are as clear as if they had happened yesterday.

Enlarged page from diary

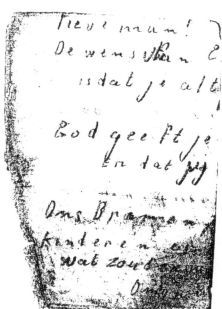

A copy of diary pages in original language.
Some words and a few pages were illegible due to the age and condition of the diary. Considering the length of the journey from Poland, to Holland, to Israel, to America and the hardships encountered, the survival of the diary intact is another miracle.
The diary size was only 2 inches by 4 inches.

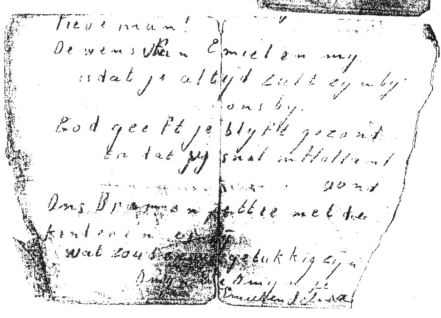

PART FIVE

Different Battles

"The meaning of awe is to realize that life takes place under wide horizons, horizons that range beyond the span of an individual life or even the life of a nation, a generation, or an era."

RABBI ABRAHAM JOSHUA HESCHEL

Liberation

We knew nothing of the outside world while we were in the loft until we began to hear the sounds of battle in mid-July, 1944. We still had no idea of the gigantic scope of the military forces or of the number of people who would lose their lives trying to rid the world of Hitler's tyranny. The vast power of the military machine that Hitler had created in Germany required the combined nations of the free world to defeat it.

We learned later how much we owed the Allies from the east and from the west. We learned how much we owed the men who fought on the beaches, in the hedgerows, in the mud and rain, in the cold and snow, in the desert, and in the Pacific. We learned of the millions who fought to save the world, but who did not live to return to their homes and families. We learned of the many who still lie in soil far from their homeland. They were from everywhere, and Chaim and I, along with all of Europe and the rest of the free world, owe these men, young and old, our lives and our freedom.

CHAPTER 19

The Liberators

As Selma and Chaim used their dreams of a normal life to survive the brutal hardships they experienced before, during, and after Sobibor, they knew nothing of the great military movements from the east and the west. These forces combined to finalize Hitler's defeat and give strength to the hopes and prayers of all who had survived the Nazi reign of terror. Millions of Jews, 'inferior' races, intellectuals, and political enemies had not survived, and those who had somehow managed to live still faced a Europe devastated by the long and bitter struggle of the Second World War.

From the West, the Allies coordinated resources and collaborated, something the Axis powers never learned to do. By late 1942, as Hitler's Final Solution approached its zenith, the Allies coordinated around the clock bombing. The RAF continued its blanket bombing of German cities by night while, by day, American planes targeted industrial centers that were important to the Nazi war effort. Long-range plans were being discussed for the invasion of a German-controlled Europe, but a military plan of that magnitude took the time and talents of numerous high-level personnel and had to be equal to the task of defeating an enemy that had brought all of Europe to its knees. There would not be a second chance.[26]

On the Eastern Front, with their failure to reach Moscow, the Germans had had the myth of their invincibility destroyed by the Russians; and at the Battle of Stalingrad, from July 7, 1942, to February 2, 1943, the German army suffered the greatest defeat it had ever known. Hitler had declared by the autumn of 1941 that the Russians were defeated, and that Leningrad (St. Petersburg) and its entire population were to be wiped from the face of the earth. He had underestimated Russia in every way, and the German armies of the Third Reich would pay heavily for these errors in judgment.

Ignoring the advice of his generals, Hitler insisted on a "Surrender is forbidden" order. All German forces, regardless of conditions or enemy strength, were to be victorious or to continue fighting until no German soldier remained alive. In spite of the coming of heavy rains, stalling men and animals in mud, followed by the snow and bitter cold of the Eastern Front, German troops were ordered to persevere for the Fatherland. With thirty-below-zero temperatures destroying men and machines and Soviet troops better prepared and trained to withstand the brutal conditions, the Germans had no choice but to admit defeat. German General Friedrich Paulus, in defiance of Hitler's express orders and in spite of having been promoted to General Field Marshall to motivate him to continue fighting, surrendered to the Soviets on January 31, 1943, to save his remaining troops.[27] With that surrender, Hitler lost the oil of the Caucasus area, badly needed for the German machines of war, and was forced to reassess the enemy he had considered defeated two years before.

Stalin had also issued "no retreat" orders for the Battle of Stalingrad. The end result was a Russian victory, but with 1.6 million combined casualties. The definitive battle on the Eastern Front was The Battle of Kursk. From July 5, 1943, to August 23, 1943, the largest concentration of military power in history took place less than two months before the escape of three hundred prisoners from Sobibor death camp.

Across a two-hundred-mile front, the Germans assembled 37 divisions with 500,000 men, 17 panzer divisions with 2,700 tanks, and over 2,000 air craft.[28] Based on intelligence of German plans, the Russians planned a strong counter-offensive. 1,300,000 Russian Red Army troops were deeply embedded in defensive positions, protected by 8,000 land mines per square mile, 3,300 tanks, 20,000 guns, and 2,500 air craft. The Soviets claimed victory with 500,000 Germans dead, wounded, or missing and eight thousand taken prisoner. Marshall Georgi Zhukov had directed the defenses of Stalingrad, Moscow, and Kursk. The Battle of

Kursk was a costly defeat for Nazi Germany's Third Reich and the last major German offensive in the East.[29]

Hitler's blind determination to defeat Russia at any cost, like his blind determination to rid Europe of Jews and other 'inferior' people at any cost, hastened the end of Germany's power on the Eastern Front and weakened German resources needed to defend the Western Front against the Allies.

As the Russian Red Army continued to move across Poland, reclaiming German-held towns and cities, they became the first Allied troops to enter a concentration camp and witness first hand the means and methods of achieving Hitler's Final Solution. When they entered Majdanek on July 23, 1944, they found that evidence of the camp's purpose was being hastily destroyed. A storehouse with 800,000 shoes had not yet been destroyed, a grim reminder of the 500,000 who had perished there.[30]

In the summer of 1944, the Soviets entered three death camps. Belzec was the first camp created for the Final Solution as part of Aktion Reinhard. It was completed in February, 1942, and received the first transports in mid-March. It was at Belzec that the system of mass murder for the Final Solution was refined. In April of 1942, Franz Stangl visited Commandant Christian Wirth (called Savage Christian by the prisoners).

In an interview with Gitta Sereny in 1971, Stangle describes the meeting, "He was standing on a hill next to the pits… the pits… full, they were all full. I can't tell you; not hundreds, thousands of corpses…oh God. That's when Wirth told me—he said that's what Sobibor was for, and that he was putting me officially in charge."[31]

In one month alone, August of 1942, 75,000 Jews were murdered at Belzec. The total killed is estimated at 434,508, but the precise number may never be known. Treblinka was open and ready to receive the first prisoners by July, 1942, and operated through October, 1943. In fifteen months of operation, 850,000 prisoners were gassed and buried in common graves or cremated.

Sobibor, where Selma and Chaim had been prisoners and where Chaim's father and brother had died in the gas chambers, was completed by March, 1942. In April of 1942, under the first Commandant, Franz Stangl, experimental gassings were conducted with 250 Jews from Krychow brought in for the test. Christian Wirth had come from Belzec to observe, and he watched through a small window until there was no longer movement among the 250 being gassed. Sobibor's methods were judged effective and became even more refined during the eighteen months of its active existence.

The job of creating a *Judenfrei* Europe was almost complete, but the escape of 300 prisoners on October 14, 1943, led by Sasha Perchersky and Leon Feldhendler, prompted the SS to destroy any evidence that the gas chamber and crematorium had ever existed. In the eighteen months of its active existence, 250,000, predominantly Jews, were victims of the Final Solution at Sobibor.

As the Russian Red Army moved across Poland, the Allies on the Western Front were preparing for the massive, coordinated invasion from across the English Channel. On June 6, 1944, after months of planning and intelligence gathering, the Normandy invasion of German-controlled Europe was launched. Successful deception by the Allies kept the Germans in the dark about the time and place of the invasion. Lack of accurate information about the Allied plans caused a critically harmful dispersion of German resources, particularly the panzer divisions.[32]

Out of touch with reality and ignoring advice from his generals, Hitler received news of the invasion and ordered that the invading forces be annihilated by nightfall on June 6, before sea and air support could arrive. Again, he underestimated his enemy.

Made up primarily of Canadian, Free French, United Kingdom, and American forces, the invasion launched nine battleships, 23 cruisers, and 104 destroyers, the largest amphibious operation in history. Within hours, Hitler's Atlantic Wall had fallen, and the Luftwaffe had been driven from the air, and the German Navy from the sea. By June 9, 1944, the initiative lay with the Allies.

D-Day was the beginning, but it took the Allies two months of brutal fighting to move inland. Unprepared for the hedgerows of Normandy, the Allies were slowed by the unfamiliar. In later weeks, Polish, Belgian, Czechoslovakian, Greek, and Dutch forces, the Australian Air Force, the New Zealand Air Force, and the Royal Norwegian Navy became involved. Of the 286,000 involved initially in the invasion, one half were U.S. and British Commonwealth forces. By the end of June over 850,000 troops, 148,000 vehicles and 570,000 tons of supplies had landed on the beaches, and by July 4, one million troops were on the German-occupied European mainland.

Conducted between June 6, and July 24,1944, the Normandy invasion by Allied forces was successful, as was the liberation of Europe that followed, but at staggering costs. Casualties for Allies on the Western Front in 1944 and 1945 numbered 776,294 dead, wounded, or missing in action. The toll for D-Day alone was 10,000 to 12,000 men, including 6,603 American lives.[33]

Field Marshall Erwin Rommel urged Hitler to consider the realities of the situation on both the Eastern and Western Fronts and to try to end the war before the German forces and the German civilian population were completely destroyed. Hitler continued his manic rages as he blamed his generals for cowardice and refused to alter his "victory or death" position.

On July 15, 1944, Rommel tried again to convince Hitler to confer with some of his field commanders for a realistic assessment of the situation facing Germany. A meeting was scheduled, but Hitler did not appear for the meeting. Rommel put his concerns in writing to the *Fuehrer*, "The troops are fighting heroically everywhere, but the unequal struggle is nearing its end." Rommel told General Hans Speidel that if Hitler did not listen to his generals and follow their advice, he would agree to join with the Operation Valkyrie conspirators to remove Hitler from power. Rommel was still opposed to assassination, but he knew that Hitler was no longer capable of being in command.[34]

Unfortunately, Operation Valkyrie was unsuccessful, and Rommel would pay for his suspected collaboration with his life.

That same month, on July 20, 1944, Selma writes in her diary that she and Chaim could hear the bombardments from their hiding place in the loft, and that Adam's brother had left his horse and household goods with Adam and Stefka because the fighting was so close to his farm. Adam told Selma and Chaim that there were many wounded German soldiers where his brother lived. Not knowing whether they would soon be free, shot by fleeing German soldiers, or caught in a counter-attack, they waited, as they had done for so long.

As the Red Army moved the German troops back across Poland, not only the fate of Selma and Chaim was at stake, but the fate of all Europe depended on an Allied victory. The battles continued.

The field commanders on the Western Front under Supreme Commander Dwight Eisenhower were Lieutenant General George S. Patton, Commander of the Third Army; General Omar Bradley, Commander of the Twelfth Army Group; and Lieutenant General Courtney Hodges, Commander of the First Army. The German forces on the Western Front faced three powerful Allied Army groups: in the north was the British 21st Army Group, commanded by Field Marshall Bernard Montgomery; in the middle, the American 12th Army Group, commanded by General Omar Bradley; and to the south, the American 6th Army Group, under the command of General Jacob L. Devers.[35]

The German army fell back, and on August 19, the French Resistance organized a general uprising to give the Allies any help they could in liberating their country. By August 25, 1944, Paris was free of German occupation for the first time in four years.

By the end of August, German armies in the West had over 500,000 casualties and had lost almost all tanks, artillery, and trucks. By September, Germany lay open to the Allied armies, but an unexplained lull occurred in the Allied offensive. Indecision about how to proceed and the difficulty of transporting supplies over 300 miles to the front were partially responsible, but strategic military differences of opinion between Field Marshall Montgomery and General Dwight Eisenhower were contributing factors.

By September, Field Marshall Montgomery (Monty) took the Canadian 1st Army and the British 2nd Army into Belgium; Brussels fell on September 3.[36] The Germans mounted a counter-attack on December 16, and with this last desperate offensive used every remaining resource available to Hitler's generals. This offensive, called the Battle of the Bulge, attempted to split the American and British forces. Aided by surprise and cold, dark, misty weather, the German offensive moved to within eight miles of the U.S. First Army headquarters.

The next day, December 17, the U.S. 101st Airborne Division arrived at Bastogne, Belgium, and occupied the town. The Germans arrived, surrounded the town, and demanded surrender, but the 101st held. As part of the Battle of the Bulge/Ardennes offensive and the hub where seven of the Ardennes mountain range roads converged, Bastogne was crucial to the outcome of the German offensive. The six-day siege by the Germans continued.

Two days before Christmas, the weather cleared and the Anglo American Air Force was cleared for attack on German supply lines, troops, and tanks. Troops strung out on the narrow, winding mountain roads of the Ardennes took heavy casualties. Three days later, General George Patton's Third Army came to the relief of the besieged 101st at Bastogne. By January 25, 1945, the Allies had pushed the Germans back to their original positions.[37]

German generals Rundstedt and Manteuffel knew the surprise offensive had been defeated and urged Hitler to withdraw. He refused to listen and, after a tirade lasting hours, screamed, "We shall yet master fate!"

The Battle of the Bulge had been costly in equipment and lives. Germany had 120,000 casualties, men killed, wounded, or missing; with 600 tanks and assault guns, 1,600 planes, and 6,000 vehicles destroyed. American losses numbered 8,000 killed, 48,000 wounded, 21,000 captured or missing, and 733 tanks destroyed.[38]

As the Allies liberated the cities, towns, and villages of France, Belgium, Luxembourg, the Netherlands, and Germany, they began to encounter the horrors of the Nazi Final Solution as they entered the concentration and extermination camps. The experiences were repeated in the east as the Russian Red Army began to liberate what was left of the camps' prisoners. In January 1945, the Soviets entered Auschwitz, a vast network of concentration and extermination camps. At Auschwitz, estimates of the victims range from 1.1 million to 2.5 million, including Selma's mother, brothers, aunts, uncles, and cousins, a total of 60 family members. Selma's family at Auschwitz and Chaim's family at Sobibor were but two families of the millions destroyed before the Allies could stop the insanity of Hitler's Final Solution and lay waste the myth of Aryan supremacy.

Numbers for the victims of each camp vary, and include not only those who were gassed and cremated, but also the thousands who died of starvation, torture, illness, individual executions, on the death trains transporting them to the camps, or, in many camps, medical experiments. Exact records of prisoners and deaths are difficult to calculate because of the sheer volume of people being transported from across Europe to various camps, the increasing insanity near the end of Hitler's reign about achieving the Final Solution, and the destruction of all evidence, records and survivors as the liberators from east and west moved to converge and destroy the Third Reich.[39]

Stunned, disbelieving, angry enough to round up nearby townspeople and make them witness the mind- numbing atrocity that had existed near them, or to invite court martials by killing remaining guards or turning them over to the surviving prisoners, the Allies liberated what was left of camp after camp.

On April 11, 1945, American troops entered Buchenwald, near Weimar, Germany, one of the first camps built and the largest because of the sub-camps attached to it. The main camp was responsible for 56,000 deaths, primarily Jews and Soviet prisoners of war.

On April 15, 1945, British forces entered Bergen-Belsen, in northwest Germany, to find hundreds of bodies unburied because of problems with the crematorium. Forty thousand prisoners were still alive, but over half of these died after the liberation because the effects of starvation, abuse, and disease were too severe to be reversed. Over 50,000 prisoners died here, including Anne Frank and her sister Margot.

American troops entered Dachau on April 29, 1945. Built in 1933, Dachau acted as a model and a training camp for what was to come. Originally built to take care of political prisoners, intellectuals, anyone who might oppose Hitler in his plans to establish Aryan Supremacy in a German-controlled Europe, Dachau's camp records recorded 206,206 prisoners and 31,951 deaths over twelve years of operation.

The liberation of Nordhausen, Mauthausen, and Gusen followed. The numbers tortured, gassed, shot, starved, beaten to death and then buried in common graves with lime sprinkled over the bodies to control the stench and to hasten decay, or cremated are unbelievable but repeatedly verified by military and civilian eye witnesses.[40]

The extent of the sadistic bestiality that had been unleashed on the prisoners at each camp shocked, sickened, and enraged even the most battle hardened Allied troops. These men had endured their own deprivations and suffering and losses. They had come through a hell that only those who have experienced battle can know, but they had never witnessed the complete breakdown of humanity as they saw it in the piles of rotting corpses and the beaten, starved, tortured remnants of what had once been recognizable as human beings.

CHAPTER 20

Memories After the War

The war was over and we were free, but the total devastation of a war-torn Europe created a different kind of prison. Millions of refugees, many recently freed from the camps, were left with no food, no money, only the clothes on their backs, and no way to get the bare necessities of life. The Allies were doing all they could to deal with a situation that, by sheer numbers, was overwhelming.

I continued to find any work I could still do, and Chaim found a job at the hospital in Chelm, but the work at the hospital was too much for him. He had experienced so much horror at Sobibor that trying to work with people who were missing arms or legs or minds was more than he could bear. Chaim was tough and strong, but there is a limit to how much suffering the human spirit can witness and endure. I was reminded again of the price my husband had paid for our survival at Sobibor.

Chaim was told to change his name and grow a mustache in order to move about more freely and safely. Jews were still in danger because non-Jews wanted to keep farms and businesses they had claimed when the owners had been sent to the camps. Leon Feldhendler, who had been a source of calm and courage at Sobibor, survived the escape that he helped to plan and lead, only to be murdered by his countrymen who were members of the Polish National Armed Forces. The family that had claimed Leon Feldhendler's home and farm when he was sent to Sobibor retained ownership after his murder.

Chaim began traveling to find what he could to help us survive. He found a woman in the Polish village of Partsifl who owned several apartments. We got one room that had no heat and no bath, but at least we had a roof over our heads. Chaim made us a rough bed from wood scraps he had gathered somehow, and we slept on straw with no blankets. One day Chaim came in with a feather bed. We felt lucky until the fleas came out that night. That was the end of our soft feather bed.

I cleaned and cleaned and cleaned. We used any kind of paper we could find to try to keep the cold and wind from coming through the windows and the holes in the walls.

Chaim continued to scavenge for necessities, and we managed to make good use of whatever he found. On one trip he found two pots, and we laughed as we tried to stuff the holes in them with bread. We then realized that the two pots had holes in different places so by putting one inside the other, we could at least cook the little food he had found or traded for.

I was afraid every time Chaim left to find food that he would be killed or that I would never see him again. The villages and woods were full of Polish Partisans, who were anti-Semitic and very dangerous. I should have had more faith in my dear husband, but I was also suffering the effects of what we had been through at Sobibor and was running short on faith in anything.

Chaim was on one of his trips when I began to feel pain in my stomach and knew it must be time for our baby to be born. After the pain started, I left a note for Chaim and walked five miles to the village, where a school was being used as a hospital. I thought when I got to the school that everything would be good. I thought I would be cared for and have help with the birth of our baby. I was wrong.

There was no welcome, no comfort, no care, and little help. The doctor had no feeling, no compassion, and told me if I didn't stop screaming, he would throw me in the street and my Jew baby could be born there. After what I had been through, I believed him. He never touched me and after days of hard labor, our baby boy was born. It was a terrible, terrible, terrible time; I can't even describe it. I was so alone and so frightened, but, more important than the loneliness or the fear was the joy. I was filled with joy that our son had been born healthy in spite of all we had been through. Holding my son in my arms, I was deeply thankful and knew that Chaim would find us. After five days Chaim came with a horse and wagon. I have no idea how he managed it, but he did. He took us home to our one room with our two pots and our bed with straw, and we named our son Emielchen Engel.

I had made clothes for the baby from what Chaim had gathered. We were so poor. Nothing—we had nothing. Chaim now had to go farther and farther to get the things we needed to live, and could be gone weeks at a time. I took care of Emielchen (our little Emiel) and cried, and then cried some more. I spoke no Polish, no Yiddish, and only a little German. None of the people in the apartments spoke Dutch. I was alone, and my loneliness seemed to have no end. It became a desperation so deep that it threatened to destroy all the hope that Chaim and I had clung to through Sobibor, through the running and hiding, and through the deprivation we were trying to survive now. I knew no way to send letters to Chaim when he was gone, but I wrote them anyway. It made me feel closer to him.

* * * * *

Selma's Letter to Chaim

> *My dearest husband,*

> *Emiel's and my wish is that you will soon be back with us. God grant that you will stay healthy and be safe.*
> *Your Selma*

* * * * *

When Chaim came home, he realized that I could not stay alone while he was traveling. Somehow, like the horse and wagon I never knew how he found, he located Ulla, my friend from the Amsterdam jail and Sobibor. She came to live with us, and I was so happy to have someone with me while Chaim was trying to find the necessities we needed to survive. Ulla had been like my little Dutch sister, and now she was staying with us and helping me care for our son. I had someone to talk to while Chaim was on his trips. The black cloud that had hung over me for weeks lifted.

Ulla had a coat and boots, so when the Russian soldiers would sing in the streets, we would trade off wearing her coat and boots to go down and hear them. They sounded so good – strong, healthy, and full of life in spite of what they had been through. Their strong voices gave us hope.

Chaim found more wood scraps and built a bed for Ulla also. We still had almost nothing, barely enough to survive; but with Ulla there and the Russian soldiers below, I felt safe. There was enough hope to last until Chaim came home.

Once Chaim came struggling up the stairs to our apartment with a live turkey. We had no idea what to do with the turkey but found we could laugh about it as the three of us figured it out. Now, we had hope and laughter and enough turkey to fill our empty stomachs. The cold kept what we didn't eat from spoiling until we could finish it. It was so cold that the pump where we got our water froze. We felt frozen much of the time, but being cold was better than having the little food we had spoil.

In spite of the hard times, we laughed many times about our struggles with that turkey, especially when we got to America and had turkey every Thanksgiving. Chaim and I agreed that none of our fine, store-bought Thanksgiving turkeys ever tasted as good as the one he, Ulla, and I cooked in that tiny, bitterly cold one-room apartment in Partsifl, Poland.

There were some public women downstairs and once some nice, friendly Russian soldiers came to our room, thinking Ulla and I were part of that group, but Chaim held up Emielchen and said, "Nyet, nyet." They bowed their heads and smiled and left.

Whatever you may hear about the brutality of Russian soldiers, we were never treated with anything but kindness and respect by any of them. From the time Sasha and his men came to Sobibor and helped plan and lead the escape, to the liberation from Adam and Stefka's hayloft, to the hard days after the liberation, they were there when we desperately needed their help. Regardless of shifting politics in the world, I will always have a soft spot in my heart for the Russian soldiers who saved us more than once.

Every day was a struggle to stay warm and to have enough food, but we had each other, our son, our friend, and our freedom.

Chaim and Saartje, with Emielchen after the liberation

CHAPTER 21

The Hardest Journey

One day Chaim came back to our apartment with news of a Dutch captain who would be willing to take us by train over Hungary and Yugoslavia to Holland and home. This was the chance we were waiting for. We could leave Poland and get back to whatever was left of my family. We boarded the train without a second thought. Wherever the train stopped, the Red Cross was there to give us food, and water to clean ourselves and Emielchen's diapers. In spite of living in better conditions, the baby and I got dysentery and had to get off the train and go to the hospital in Chenoviz, Hungary.

Everywhere there were people—many still in concentration camp clothes—looking for a way to survive long enough to build a new life, or to determine if there were any pieces of their old life left. Heartache and sadness seemed to be a part of every life now. The war was over, but the devastating effects of Hitler's insanity continued to destroy.

Chaim came to the hospital where Emielchen and I were recovering from dysentery. Still sick and very weak, I didn't think we could travel, but the train was ready to leave and could wait for no one. This was the only way for us to get to Odessa and on the boat back to Holland. Sick or not, we had to go. I lost track of how long it took us to get to Odessa, but I clung to the thought that at least we were going in the right direction.

When we did arrive in Odessa, the Red Cross was amazing. The city was dark, all black and gray, but the way we were treated made it all seem wonderful. We were given good food and clothes for us and our son. Our excitement grew; we were one step closer to Holland and home. In Odessa, for the first time in years, we didn't have to live in fear. We were fed and clothed and cared for. We were at peace.

We stayed in Odessa three months, time for our minds and bodies and souls to heal from the constant fear and hardship of the last two years. For the first time in over two years we were not threatened by Nazis SS, or Ukrainian guards, or scabies, or rats, or hunger, or cold, or lack of medicine. We were at peace but anxious about what we would find when we reached my home. We began to believe even more strongly that our enduring hope for freedom and our dream of being able to share a normal life were getting closer to becoming our reality. Our joy was boundless! We were free, we were healthy, we had a new son, and we were headed for my home in Zwolle, where we hoped and prayed we would find my brother Bram and his family alive.

When it was time to leave Odessa, we learned that only Dutch citizens would be allowed to return to Holland. The captain of the ship told Chaim not to speak and he would board him as one of the Dutch passengers because of his marriage to me. To have come so far, and endured so much just to be separated now was unthinkable. The captain told us to use my maiden name and for me to answer all questions for the family. Chaim could now understand and speak Dutch, but he did not sound like someone from the Netherlands. Thankful for the captain's help, I carried our son, held my Chaim's hand, as always, and walked up the gangplank.

Only those who have thought they would never see their home again can know how we felt. In spite of everything we had been through, or maybe because of it, we were overcome with joy. We were going home! Holland would be Chaim's home too. We could not stay in the land of Sobibor, Auschwitz, and countless other places of suffering and death, so Chaim was going to my home. It would become our home.

Before the captain spoke to Chaim about his plans for keeping us together, I became so fearful about Chaim not being able to go to Holland with me, of our being separated after all we had been through, that I was nervous enough to stop my milk. I could no longer nurse Emielchen as I had done since his birth. A nurse on board kindly took our baby, our little Emiel to get some milk for him. I should never have let her take him; but we had been treated with such kindness, and I knew she was trying to help us. I would not have known any more than she did that the milk she gave Emiel was contaminated, but at least I would have been there. Maybe my mother's instincts would have warned me. I don't know. I do know that our precious baby boy, who was now the biggest part of our dreams for a future and a normal life, became sick from the bad milk and died in my arms. This time I prayed not to live, but to die. I prayed that the pain would kill me.

The Dutch captain wrapped our tiny son in a white cloth, gathered everyone around, read a ceremony from the ship's manual and then slipped our precious Emielchen into the sea. People were so kind. They tried to get through my grief to offer comfort, but I could feel nothing except the pain of a suffering greater than any I had ever known. It was a numbing grief that threatened my sanity and destroyed my will to live. I did not know then, and I still don't know how we survived this, our greatest loss. But somehow we did. At times I could not try or even pretend that I wanted to go on. Chaim would hold me, rocking me gently back and forth, and tell me how happy our Emielchen had been the last three months of his life. I clung to that thought. I had always grieved for the mothers who had their children taken from them at Sobibor. Now I knew the depth of that grief. There are no words to describe it. Chaim suffered as much as I did over the loss of our son, but his quiet strength and our love helped us survive our greatest loss. Nothing we had endured could equal the pain of losing our son just as we were getting close to our dream.

The father of Anne Frank was on the same boat, but after our precious Emiel's death, we were beyond talking. As was he. What words can be spoken in the depths of a despair so deep that there is only darkness?

We were eight days on the boat, everyone was so sick we could just lie on the deck. In Marseille, they made us a big dinner and the French were very kind to us. All had suffered so much with the occupations and the camps. I am still amazed that kindness survived anywhere, but it continued to surface at the least expected times and in the most unexpected ways. Just when I doubted the existence of human kindness in the damaged world that remained, a person or an event would prove that kindness in people still existed in spite of or maybe because of everything that had been done to destroy it.

Chaim always said that he believed in the fundamental goodness of human beings, and that to change that would be allowing the Nazi regime of Hitler and its atrocities to determine his beliefs. He refused to allow them to take his beliefs from him, as they had taken his family. I, on the other hand, believe in the goodness of some, but have never been able to understand the evil of others. I wonder even now if goodness and evil are not almost evenly matched in a tenuous battle, each winning occasional bouts within nations and individuals. I do believe that love and kindness occasionally triumph or Chaim and I would not have survived to tell our story. And I know, with all the certainty of my being, that love is the only force powerful enough to endure and defeat the evil that can exist in the darkest human hearts.

CHAPTER 22

Coming Home

When we finally got to Zwolle, I walked toward our hotel, frightened about what we might find but hoping and praying that my brother Bram and his family would be there. My smile was so big and my fears so strong that I couldn't make the whistle our family had used to signal a return home. When I was finally able to get the whistle out, my brother Bram and his wife Jettie and their children, whom I didn't even know about, came running out of the hotel with disbelief and then joy on their faces.

There had been no way for us to contact each other, so Bram thought that his little sister had suffered the same fate as our mother and our other two brothers. He never expected to see me again, and his surprise was total when I introduced Chaim as my husband.

We had such a mixture of joy and sadness; the heartache came first, and then the joy. We were so happy to find that at least two members of my family had survived and that we would be together again, but the sadness returned and overcame the joy as we talked about the fate of the rest of our family and Chaim's. We had learned in Poland that no one in Chaim's family had survived the camps, and now I learned that only Bram, Jettie, their children, and I had survived in our family. I was glad the children were too young to understand what we were talking about. Bram, Jetti, and their children had been hidden by a family near Zwolle. Again, I had proof that kindness still existed in our world.

When Bram showed me our mother's picture, I broke down completely. She had thrown it off the train on the way to Auschwitz after writing a message to her children on the back. The Dutch Underground had recovered it and returned it to Bram. My mother, who had lived her life with nothing but gentleness and love in her heart, had been trying to reach her children to comfort them even on the way to her death. I couldn't bear to think of my mother, Alida Nathan Wijnberg, the kindest, gentlest person I had ever known, dying as a result of Hitler's madness, and never being a part of my life again. I never had a chance to say good-bye, or tell her how much I loved, respected and admired her, or thank her for the years of happiness she had given all of us. Seeing my mother's picture made the loss of all my loved ones seem more than I could bear. Again, Chaim held me while I shed my tears for my mother and brothers, our son, and the rest of my family and his.

After the Germans were defeated and the occupation was over in Holland, Bram and Jettie had moved back into the hotel and opened it for business. Everyone was trying to return to normal as soon as possible. I was home, but it was terrible because Bram, Jettie, and their children were the only survivors from our whole family. Being home again made me miss my mother and other two brothers even more. My memories of our happy life and what we had lost were almost more painful than the ones I had while at Sobibor. Then, uncertainty of my family's fate had left at least a glimmer of hope that they had survived and that we would be together again. Of the sixty members of my family who had died in the camps, we were never able to get any details of their deaths. But that may have been better. My nightmares would have been even worse if they had been based on fact.

The hardships we had suffered and survived at Sobibor, in Stefka and Adam's barn loft, on the train to Odessa, and on the boat taking us to Holland were nothing compared to the loss of our little Emielchen and now my mother and brothers and all of Chaim's family. Once again, Chaim was my rock. He was suffering the same losses, but his love and concern for me and his faith in our future helped us both heal.

Saartje visiting Chaim while he is hiding in Amsterdam

Saartje's mother, Alida Nathan Wijnberg

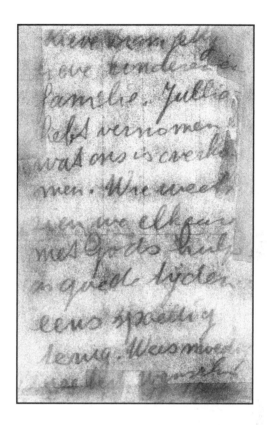

Saartje's mother, Alida Nathan Wijnberg, threw her picture from the train on the way to Auschwitz. The Dutch Underground recovered it and returned it to Bram. She had written a message to her children on the back.

The message reads:
Dear Bram and Jettie,

Dear Children,
You hear about what has happened to us. We wait. Who knows if we ever see each other again. With God's help we see each other in better times again.
Be strong and be brave, my children. We will meet at a better time.

Best Wishes,
Love,
Your Mother

Chaim and Saartje's identification papers after their return to Holland

CHAPTER 23

No Longer My Home

After we had been back in Zwolle almost a year, our daughter Lidi was born. She was named Alida after my precious mother, who would never have a chance to hold or get to know her granddaughter. Lidi's birth moved us both beyond the grief that had almost defeated us. When we held her tiny body and looked at how perfect she was, we knew that our most important step toward the normal life we had dreamed of had been taken.

The hotel was doing well, but the times were very hard. Everyone in Holland and the rest of Europe was doing whatever was necessary to rebuild destroyed homes, businesses, and lives. Our hotel had been a thriving business before the Germans came. Now with all of us working together, Hotel Wijnberg became very successful again. But for reasons I didn't understand, the hotel and Zwolle no longer felt like my home. We had to register with the police, still using my maiden name because only Dutch citizens were allowed to remain in the Netherlands. All citizens coming back into the country had to be quarantined. This was my home, my country, and yet my husband and I could not use our real name and had to be quarantined! Diseases were rampant because of conditions during and after the war; they had to be contained as part of rebuilding what had been lost. I understood the reasons for all these actions, but it still hurt. Official word then came that all Polish people had to return to Poland. We couldn't believe that would happen, but I told Chaim that if it came to that, I would go with him. We promised each other that we would never be separated, and no new rules, laws, or policies could change that promise. We had lived by other people's senseless laws for too long. We would find a way to stay together. To prepare for staying with

Chaim if he had to go back to Poland, I gave up my Dutch citizenship. I later regretted this decision, but at the time it seemed the only way I would be allowed to go with him wherever he went, and that was the most important thing. Our staying together and sharing a normal life was all that mattered to me.

We were finally able to get "officially" married in 1945. We had always considered ourselves married; but as soon as the officials in Zwolle who could perform the service came back from England, we were legally joined as man and wife. We both knew we had been man and wife for over two years in our hearts.

My beautiful Zwolle was not a good place for Chaim and me now. We had survived Sobibor, only to be persecuted by the laws of my own country. My home was no longer my home, not the place I had grown up and loved so. Nothing was as it had been before the war.

We waited for the next three months to hear about the deportation order, with Chaim staying in hiding most of the time. The war was over, the Germans had lost, and here we were, still in hiding just as before. I was angry and bitter that my countrymen could treat its citizens so badly after all we had been through. Survivors from Sobibor came to our rescue. They had become experts after the escape at hiding, and now helped Chaim hide while we waited to see what would happen about the deportation orders.

The orders for all Polish people to return to Poland never materialized, but the damage had been done to my love for my country. How could a rule so callous as to divide a man from his wife and child be fair or just? I had had enough of questions with no answers from the days of Hitler's madness.

With the good news of the deportation orders being cancelled came also the happy event of the birth of our son. Fredrick Engel was born in 1948; little Freddie completed our family. I was saddened that he would never know his older brother, Emielchen Engel, but he brought total joy with his birth to Chaim and me and his big sister Lidi. This was my family. We would find our home.

For personal and business reasons, Chaim and I decided to give our part of the hotel to Bram and Jettie and build a business and a life of our own. We met a man with an empty store, and Chaim started a men's clothing store with custom tailoring. He did well for awhile, but there was so little money that people bought only necessities. We got out with the money we had put in it but had to start over once again.

Still Chaim dreamed of going to America, and I just wanted to leave Holland. Chaim and I agreed that this was not our home, not this place where we couldn't use our real name, and where Chaim had to be in hiding as we had been after the escape from Sobibor. We knew we would find our real home, but Holland could not be our home. My home was wherever Chaim and Lidi and Fred were, and where we had the best chance to live the dreams that had helped us survive.

CHAPTER 24

Searching for a Home

We couldn't get papers for America, so in 1951, we decided to go to Israel. I had always wanted to go to Israel; for me, it was a bigger dream than America. I saw Israel as a way to leave behind all the fears and deprivations caused by prejudice and hatred against Jews. In Israel, my Promised Land, everyone was Jewish. I was happy; but I knew that for my dear husband, it was only a temporary move that kept him from having to return to Poland. More importantly, Israel was a move that gave us time to get papers and find a way to get to America. We sold the few things we had and prepared to start over again. For now, our future was in Israel, but I think we both knew it was not forever.

This time we did have some things to take with us. We took as much food and as many clothes as we could; we had learned through hard experience that those were the only true essentials during the hard times—that and being together. We also knew we could sell what we didn't need after we got there.

Arriving in Israel, we soon found a house in Nafala. The house was primitive, with no electricity, but everyone on the kibbutz lived the same way. I loved it, but Chaim hated the kibbutz, and the work that had to be done. He was a hard worker, but he hated working in the field, picking grapes and apples, and feeding chickens. He felt he was a business man working like a farmer. He had done that before, and my Chaim was not one who ever wanted to go backwards. He looked to the future and moved forward. He finally found a job in a village not far from our home. He worked as a waiter and I worked as a cleaning lady or in the fields. We did anything and everything we could do to make a little money. In spite of Chaim's unrealized dream of America, we were living closer to our dream of a normal life than we ever had. We had our perfect Lidi and little Fred and enough to get by. We had our freedom, and I was happy.

A friend who knew of Chaim's unhappiness with the farm work told Chaim about a lady who was leaving for America, and that he should take over her vegetable store. As always, Chaim saw the potential and took the opportunity. It was very hard work, up at 4 am to get the vegetables and then to open the store and keep it open late enough to get every customer, but he loved it. He was in business for himself.

My Chaim was a good, hard working, honest man, one that people knew they could trust. As a result, he did so well with the little vegetable store that in five years he had four markets in four towns. He was so busy that he had to give out numbers for the customers.

We were free; we had Lidi and Fred and each other; we were leading a normal life. This had been our dream for so many years, the dream that had kept us going. Now, we were living beyond our dreams, with good neighbors and great friends. We went to concerts and dances, and I was happier than I had ever been in my life. Our dreams from Sobibor and Adam and Stefka's hay loft and Zwolle were being lived, but I knew deep in my heart that Chaim's true dream had not yet been realized.

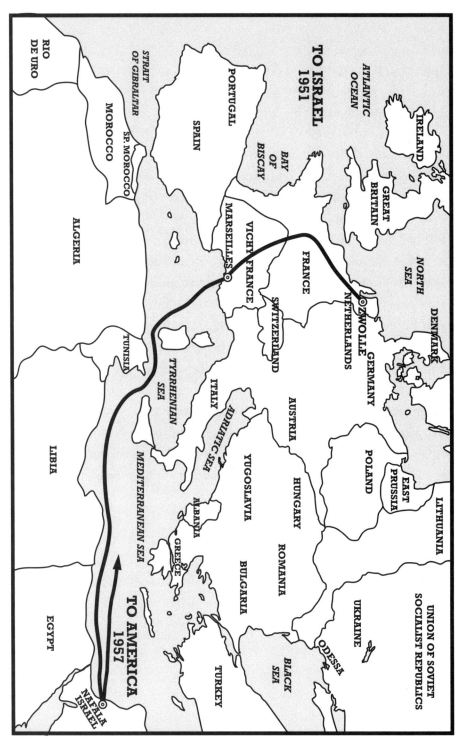

Zwolle, Netherlands to Nafala, Israel; Israel to America

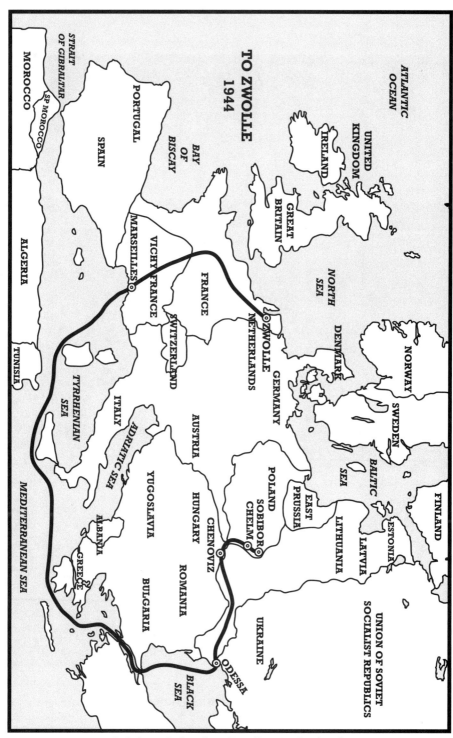

Sobibor, Poland to Zwolle, Netherlands

Chaim, Saartje, Lidi and Freddie in Israel

CHAPTER 25

Chaim's Dream

And then, Chaim's miracle that he had waited for so long happened. My uncle, a doctor who had immigrated to Israel before the beginning of the war, went to America. After several weeks, he and his wife contacted us with unbelievable news. They had found a lawyer in Buffalo who could help us get our papers for immigrating to America! Chaim was in heaven, and there was never any question that we would once again start over. This time, we would start over in America, always the land of my husband's dreams. So, in 1957, we were going to become Americans. Chaim was 42 and I was 35.

My husband was a very calm man, but now he couldn't contain his excitement. I had never seen him in such a hurry to pack and get started. Chaim's dream of so many years was coming true, and that meant everything to me. We sold the little we had, packed, and left our normal life in Israel. We went first to Italy, where we spent two weeks, and then by boat to America. We were on the water four weeks and most of that time at least one or often all of us were seasick.

In spite of the rough passage and facing the unknown, Chaim felt that this was the dream that had brought us through everything. What he had been so determined to have for both of us was now in our grasp. It didn't bother him that we knew no one, had very little to start with, and had already started over so many times. He was as certain we would build a good life in America as he had been that we would escape Sobibor, and someday live a normal life together.

After four weeks of seasickness, we arrived in Westport, Connecticut. I had never seen such riches, even before the war in Holland. The grocery stores amazed me, the department stores even more so. There was so much of everything that choices had to be made constantly. I occasionally thought of the times we had nothing, absolutely nothing, and now we had access to everything. America had not been my dream but this new country was amazing, and it was Chaim's dream. That made it mine too.

We stayed with the lawyer and his wife for a week. In spite of their home being very crowded with both families, it was wonderful. I had never met nicer people, and I thought about my fears from years ago that all kindness had disappeared from the world. Once again, we were being met with the greatest of kindness from people we didn't even know.

After much looking, we found our first American home. We called it our "brown" apartment. It had brown floors, brown walls, brown everything and was so dirty that it took me one month of hard scrubbing to really get it clean. But it was ours and we were happy.

Even before he became successful, Chaim was as happy as he had always known he would be in his new home. His dream had brought us here; this was where we belonged. I loved it as much as he did, but Israel was still close to my heart.

Chaim worked for a short time in a fine grocery store, Christidy, and then we saved enough to buy an Arnold's Bread delivery franchise. After six months Chaim sold the franchise and bought a Hallmark Greeting Card store. Everything we did was hard work with long hours, but everything Chaim did paid off. He was the business person, but I was always there, cleaning, waiting on customers, doing whatever I could to help people and to build our success.

Fred and Lidi had spoken only Hebrew when we arrived in Connecticut, but they picked up English quickly. They had had to adjust so many times that we hated to ask them to adjust again, by changing not only schools and friends, but countries as well. We shouldn't have worried because Chaim's enthusiasm was so great it was contagious, and Fred and Lidi were equal to the challenge of adjusting to this new home. By the end of the first year, they were speaking almost accent-free English. I, even after all these years, still speak English with a heavy Dutch accent, or so I have been told.

Lidi and Fred adjusted to Connecticut more quickly than I did, and Chaim felt as if this was where he was always meant to be. Not one time were we ever homesick for Poland or Holland or Israel. He was home, so I was home too.

Lidi and Fred never wanted to hear about the hard times that Chaim and I had shared in Sobibor and afterwards. I think on one hand it hurt them to know what we had been through, and on the other hand it made them feel different. Like all children of immigrants, they had to leave a little of the old behind for a while to adjust fully to the new. We understood.

Chaim and I have always been proud of our children and now grandchildren and great grandchildren. All have been successful in whatever they have chosen to do, and, more importantly, they are good, caring people, our greatest legacy and worth everything we went through so many years ago to follow our dream.

Dreams
Realized

Saartje's 70th birthday gathering with Chaim, children, grandchildren
and members of her brother Bram's family from Canada

Living the normal life of their dreams

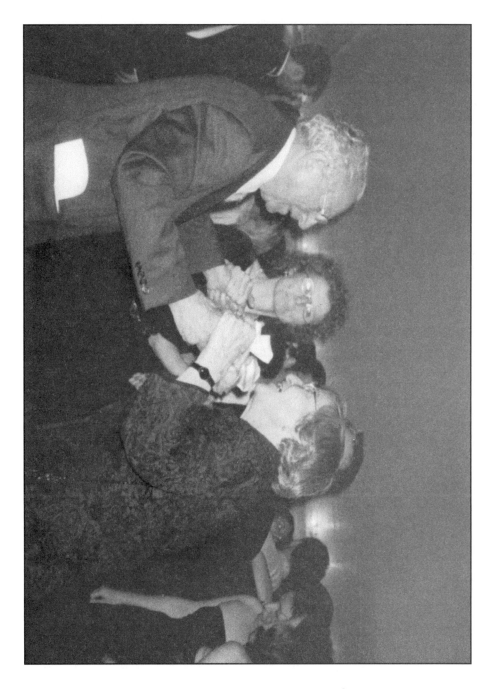

Saartje and Chaim's last dance at a granddaughter's
wedding shortly before his death

CHAPTER 26

Speaking Out

Soon after we got settled in America, Chaim and I began speaking to schools, churches, synagogues, civic organizations, everywhere but street corners, and we were willing to do that too. We spoke anywhere we could get an audience that wanted to hear about the result of allowing prejudice and hatred to go unchecked, and how our love had helped us survive Hitler's most efficient death camp.

When we were offered money, we refused it. One survivor was getting $5,000 for every appearance. We always felt our speaking out about our experiences was small payment for our survival. We appreciated the opportunity and assumed the responsibility of speaking for those who could no longer speak for themselves. It was our small way of honoring all who had died as a result of this insane period of history.

Our favorite audiences were the high school groups. They were more interested than we ever thought they would be and horrified by "man's inhumanity to man," as they often quoted to us. As teenagers, they were also very interested in hearing how our love for each other helped us survive, and how each of us is responsible for taking a personal stand against prejudice and injustice. I still have hundreds of notes that came to us from the high school students who had been touched by our story and wanted advice on how they could help in the fight against prejudice and injustice. We responded by telling them to talk to teachers, parents, and fellow students and start awareness programs.

Our audiences and the notes and letters they sent meant to us that people cared about the suffering that had been a part of so many lives. Many wrote of personal responsibility being the only way to defeat prejudice whenever and wherever it begins. One letter stated that each person must be willing to stand against evil before it rises to full power on the wings of apathy. I liked that. I also liked that many did start awareness programs to help at least identify comments and behavior that belittled anyone, or laughter that was at another's expense because of what that person was born to be.

All this time, Chaim was doing very well in business. He found a buyer for our greeting card store and then bought a jewelry store. We started fairly small but built it steadily until we were doing almost as much with our expensive gift items as we were with the diamonds and other jewelry. We had started over so many times, and each time Chaim had made a success of whatever we were doing. I was not surprised that Engel's Jewelry became another of our success stories.

When the call came in the mid-1960s asking us to testify at the trials being held for some of the Sobibor guards, we immediately agreed. The trip to Haagen, Germany, was long, but we felt that at last justice was being done, and we wanted to be a part of that. We knew it would be hard to relive the atrocities we had experienced and witnessed, but we knew that many of the people responsible were still enjoying their freedom after they had taken it from thousands in the cruelest ways possible.

We made three trips to testify, but the sentences were usually so light for what had been done that we didn't accept a fourth invitation. It seemed that too many just got slaps on the hand for their involvement, and then even that became a commuted sentence. Gustav Wagner was discovered living peacefully in Brazil. Even after proof of his service at Sobibor and his admission of having been there, Brazil refused to extradite him to Germany, Poland, or Israel. According to him, he had just been following orders like any good military man. He supposedly committed suicide, but I don't think he was the kind of man who would commit suicide. I hope he was killed by someone who had been at Sobibor or who had lost their family there. That would be true justice.

Karl Frenzel was sentenced to life in prison but served only a few years before his sentence was commuted. Others who had been guards received only three- or four-year sentences. It seemed that the courts were as anxious to be done with Sobibor as the Germans had been when they tried to cover it with grass and trees.

* * * * *

After we had been in the United States six years, Lidi came to us with the man she wanted to marry. Chaim and I were excited that our daughter had found someone she wanted to spend her life with and gave her an especially big wedding, maybe to make up for the one Chaim and I never had. Our children could have all the things we could only dream of for so many years, and we, like all parents, wanted them to have everything. We hoped that Lidi would be as happy in her marriage as Chaim and I had been in ours.

Unfortunately, that was not to be. Chaim and I hated that the happiness we had shared was not to be our daughter's as well. Their marriage did last long enough to create two beautiful children, our precious granddaughters. Just before the divorce, Lidi and her husband had built a house in Branford, Connecticut. Now, Chaim and I decided that Branford would be a good place for us to live also. It was not just to be near Lidi and the grandchildren, but that was one of the major reasons. It proved to be a good decision in every way. I am still in the same house; it holds too many wonderful memories for me to ever want to live anywhere else. Lidi found her great love several years after the divorce and is now married to him. Chaim and I were thrilled.

One of our great joys came when our granddaughter Tagan graduated from college and wanted to retrace the route that Chaim and I had taken at the beginning—from Zwolle, Holland, my original home, to Brudzew, Poland, Chaim's original home, to Sobibor, where we met, to Israel and then back home to Branford, Connecticut and America. It always touched us when people cared about our story and its message, but it was beyond belief that our granddaughter cared enough to do this.

Fred found the woman he wanted to spend his life with, and is still as much in love with her as ever. They added two more beautiful granddaughters to our family. Next to freedom and surviving to share a normal life, Chaim and I shared the dream of having our children as happy and as in love as we had always been. That dream has also come true.

Chaim retired in 1989 at 73, and we began to travel even more than we had before. With two big trips a year, we were soon seeing all the places we had been before, and added Greece, China, Japan, and anywhere the mood took us. When we were home, we went into New York often for the opera, ballet, or shows. My beloved husband and I were living a life beyond anything we could ever have imagined in Sobibor.

In Sobibor, 'normal' meant just being free to live, and work, and raise a family. Our 'normal' in America was so much more than our dreams that we had to pinch ourselves to be sure we were awake and not in the middle of a dream about a life that could never be ours. This life was ours, and it was not a dream; but we never stopped appreciating our new normal life or being aware that freedom and a good life are not to be taken for granted.

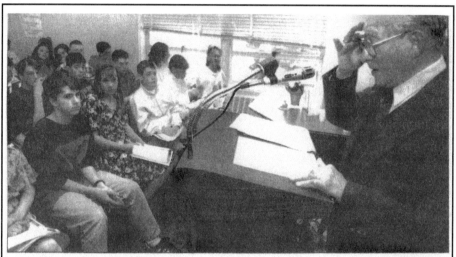

Peter Casolino/Register

Former concentration camp prisoner Chaim Engel relates his Holocaust camp stories to middle school students in Milford.

Holocaust was real, survivors tell students

By Susette J. Burton
Register Staff

MILFORD

MILFORD — Selma and Chaim Engel, survivors of the Nazi extermination camp Sobibor, still have the scars and memories wrought by the Holocaust.

The elderly couple spoke on Monday at East Shore Middle School's Holocaust Remembrance Day program, which is tied in to an interdisciplinary unit on Prejudice Reduction-Holocaust Education taught at the school.

Selma Engel, who met her husband at Sobibor, was born in Holland.

Chaim Engel was born in Lodz, Poland. Chaim was a soldier in the Polish army and survived a German prison camp. In 1942 he was brought to Sobibor, where his job was to separate the clothes of people sent to the gas chamber.

The couple survived the Oct. 14, 1943, uprising at Sobibor and escaped. After the war, they went

to Holland and then to Israel and later immigrated to the United States.

The Holocaust was the systematic, bureaucratic annihilation of 6 million Jews by the Nazi regime during World War II.

The Engels told students of the horrors of life in Sobibor, where they lived in fear that each day would be their last. More importantly, they helped shine the spotlight on how destructive intolerance can be.

"They slaughtered us like animals in a slaughterhouse. It's just incomprehensible that something like this could have happened," said Chaim Engel. "Let's hope that things like that can never happen again."

The couple said they have never returned to Sobibor, which was dismantled in late 1943 with no trace of its existence. A monument marks the location. By the end of the war in 1945, only

about 50 Jews survived Sobibor while about 250,000 Jews were murdered in the camp, according to reports.

Selma Engel, whose mother and two of her brothers and all of her aunts and uncles were murdered in Auschwitz, said she cannot fathom how people can claim the Holocaust never happened.

"How come I came back after the war and had no family left if there was no Holocaust?" she asked.

Every day was a nightmare, the couple said.

"I couldn't understand how I was walking around Sobibor while everyone around me was dying. It was like a dream," Selma Engel said.

Caitlin McAlpine, a seventh-grader taking the course on prejudice reduction, said the couple had a tremendous effect on students.

"They gave us a better understanding of the Holocaust. It's better hearing it from real people

not just reading about it," said Caitlin.

She said the class has taught students "to not really be prejudiced and to try and prevent this from happening again."

The course is designed to help students acquire a sensitivity and a tolerance of each other as well as teaching them to appreciate and to respect individual differences.

"It was more powerful to hear what they lived through. Books don't always tell us everything," said Lindsay Davies.

A show titled "Performances for Life: Holocaust-Inspired Art" will be at the Jewish Community Center in Woodbridge Thursday.
Page B2

A Lifetime Commitment ...

A lifetime commitment continues with *Dancing Through Darkness*

Early visit to record Selma's memories

Presenting a copy of *Dancing Through Darkness*
to Selma for her 91st birthday

The Commitment continues as author speaks.
Photo courtesy of Belmont University, Nashville, Tennessee

Speaking to groups of all ages about the dangers of good people
remaining silent in the presence of prejudice and injustice.
Fourth graders at Holy Rosary Academy, Donelson, Tennessee

Interview by John Seigenthaler on NPT's *A Word on Words*

CHAPTER 27

Our Last Dance

When Chaim became sick, I thought he would be fine because he always had been. Even when he required dialysis, I thought he would get well. We had not had enough time together. Our love had lasted 61 years, but it was not enough. When he finally reached the point that I knew he was never going to be well again, my heart broke and has never healed.

I used to sit beside him, even when he was not fully conscious, and beg him not to die. "Chaim," I would plead over and over, "Chaim, please don't die. How can I live without you? I can't live without you. I don't know how. Please don't die." I held his hand while I talked to him and begged him to stay with me. He always had before, but this time he couldn't. I was holding his hand for the last time when his fingers didn't return the pressure of mine. I just sat very still, continuing to hold his hand and hoping that somehow this time too he would take me with him.

My Chaim was gone. I don't know how I stood it then, or how I stand it now. I did not think I could live without him by my side. He was my life. I knew that I did not want to live without him but that, somehow, I had to learn how to face life without my Chaim there to hold my hand.

I had done impossible things before in my life, but he had always been there to hold my hand and make me stronger. He held my hand when he told me to keep my head up but think of other places when we had to watch the brutal punishments at roll call in Sobibor. He held it as he somehow cared for me and saved me from the gas chamber during my bout with typhus. He held it as he coaxed me to eat in spite of food like garbage, so we could both stay strong enough to survive. He clung to my hand during the escape from Sobibor, and he continued to cling to it as he made me run when I could run no more and begged to give up.

He worked with Adam and Stefka to get more food for me when we found out I was pregnant. Somehow, he found a horse and wagon to bring Emielchen and me home from the hospital. In the middle of war-ravaged Europe, he found my friend, Ulla, to come live with us so I would not be alone with our baby while he scavenged for the bare necessities to keep us alive. He held and comforted me when our Emielchen had died and been buried at sea. We had everything, as long as we were together. Now my love, my life, was gone.

I did not think I could bear this pain. The numbness of a dark and endless grief held me until I couldn't breathe and didn't want to. After months of grieving and not being able to function as well on my own as I needed to, my children suggested that I talk to someone to see if that would help me rise from my grief. I don't think my sessions are lessening my grief, but I do in a way enjoy them because I am able to tell someone who didn't know him all about my Chaim and our life together. I am able to tell the doctor how Chaim never looked back, how he always knew we would get out of Sobibor, survive the hardest times, and stay together to enjoy the good times. I am able to talk about how he was the most positive person I have ever known, how he was ashamed of having to kill another human being during the escape, how the things he had to do for our survival destroyed a part of him he could never retrieve. Always he said, "We will make it." To him, this was a simple statement of fact.

He always believed we were no better, no smarter, and tried no harder than the millions who perished. I think we both felt we owed it to those who were not able to survive to tell their story as often and as accurately as we could as long as we lived. I am able to tell the doctor how Chaim loved *The New York Times,* and how he read it completely every day, how he could study a language a few weeks before we went to any country and learn enough for us to get by, how he was always Mr. Engel to our customers, how he always wore a suit and tie, and how completely he loved me and his family and his adopted country.

Men like my Chaim don't come along very often, and I have finally decided that one way to honor his life and our love is to continue to speak and write about how our love defeated the worst atrocities the mind of man could devise. He would be really put out with me if I didn't try to live as full a life as possible and share what our experiences taught us. I talk about my life with Chaim to the doctor and now I smile more than I cry.

That would make my husband proud.

E4 Saturday, July 12, 2003 / The Atlanta Journal-Constitution

Engel, hero of WWII breakout

BRANFORD, CONN.

Chaim Engel, 87, who helped organize a group escape from a Nazi death camp, died July 4 in New Haven, Conn.

During World War II, Mr. Engel was a prisoner at Sobibor, a secret death camp in eastern Poland, where 250,000 people, chiefly Jews, were murdered. On Oct. 14, 1943, 300 prisoners escaped in an uprising that involved killing guards and camp officers. Only 50 of those who escaped survived until the end of the war.

Partly because of his good health, Mr. Engel was

Chaim Engel escaped a Nazi death camp with hundreds of others, including his future wife.

assigned to sort through clothing of doomed prisoners; among them he found his brother's belongings. Once, when the Nazis executed every 10th man standing in a line, he was No. 9.

The woman Mr. Engel eventually married, Selma Wyn-

berg, arrived at Sobibor in spring 1943 in a group of Dutch Jews. They met when guards forced prisoners to dance for their amusement, and he began looking out for her. He had one goal, to leave the camp holding her hand.

The couple hid in a Polish farmer's hayloft for nine months and found their way to Holland.

Mr. Engel, insisting he was no hero, said a man can do a lot of things to save his life. But his wife proudly said, "He was the only man who took his girlfriend along."

— New York Times

Chaim's Obituary, the begining of the search for the rest of his story

CHAPTER 28

Reflections

Our past cannot die while we live. It lingers at the edge of memory, ready to bring back joys once known. The gentle memories come easily and cling to their time in the present, making us smile; but the nightmares of the past, neither gentle nor patient, demand their full due in spite of futile attempts to keep them silent. They come un-summoned to torment us with the anguish of suffering and loss we wish never to recall. And, yet, we do…over and over again.

Sobibor could not destroy the dreams that Chaim and I had, nor could it determine what we became after we survived the hell they had created. It did not make us lose our faith in the ultimate goodness of most people, nor did it destroy our laughter forever. At Sobibor, we experienced what the darkest night of a man's soul can create, but at this same tortured, tormented time and place, we also witnessed unbelievable acts of courage and sacrifice. In the depths of depravity and despair, we felt hope come alive, as we found a love that lasted over sixty years and gave us a life far beyond anything we could have dreamed.

The scope of the Holocaust Chaim and I and millions of others experienced is unique in recorded history. The evil of prejudice and injustice that created the unspeakable horrors of that time is not.

Then, I felt that no one else had suffered as I had. Now I know that millions faced that evil or others, suffered beyond endurance, and did not survive to bear witness. Chaim always refused the description of hero for his part in the escape from Sobibor and considered us only a small part in all that happened in the madness of that time. I know that evil incarnate claimed the balance of power during much of my early life, but evil, in different forms, is present and powerful in our world today. Good and evil coexist and remain in constant battle, the balance of power always tenuous at best. I know that evil on any level can be weakened and even defeated by love, faith, courage, hope, or dreams—all the best of what it means to be wonderfully human.

The evil of prejudice and injustice has been and always will be present and powerful, but it is not invincible. Each of us must play a part, no matter how small, in helping the good, the pure, and the sacred triumph

When I last read my diary, I was shamed by my many complaints and often narrow views. My list of complaints was endless and boring. I apologize now for relating such a self-centered, spoiled story of that time in my life. I was young in years and in experience, and I judged everything only by how it affected me. In my mind, I was the center of the world.

I wrote harshly of Stefka during the nine cruel months Chaim and I were hidden in the Nowak's barn loft. She burned my only coat after telling me over and over that the oven would only kill the lice, not harm the coat. She rarely gave us enough food and water. She took the little money we had and then didn't buy the medicine we desperately needed. She even kept one pair of Chaim's socks when he only had two. Now, as an adult and a survivor, I realize that Stefka lived in paralyzing fear of discovery the whole nine months Chaim and I were hidden. Our discovery by the SS troops still searching for Sobibor escapees would have meant certain death for Adam, Stefka, their son, and possibly other family members and friends. My Chaim always thought, above all, that we owed Adam and Stefka our lives and undying gratitude for their willingness to risk everything to hide us. I now know he was right.

I knew that Adam wanted to help us hide, but that Stefka had agreed only to get the money Chaim had hidden in bandages wrapping his legs. That discovery, not kindness, prompted the decision that allowed us to hide in their barn. She agreed only to get a share of what we had risked our lives to steal and hide at Sobibor. I saw her greed as taking what we would need to survive when the war was over. What seemed like pure greed at that time I see now as a desperate effort to feed her son and save her family. The times were terrible for everyone; survival was a constant struggle. The money that we gave Adam and Stefka for risking their lives and their son's life to hide us might have helped them survive the brutality and deprivation of that war-damaged time and place. The money could keep them from starving for a while longer. It could not prevent their being reported by neighbors, or discovered by German troops and shot for sheltering Jews.

Chaim could always talk to Stefka and get her help with more food and medicine when the situation seemed hopeless. I blamed it then on her not liking me, but now I know that she responded to Chaim because he treated her like the very important person she was, a fellow human being. I built great high walls trying to force her to see everything my way. Chaim understood her justifiable fears for her family and the depth of their poverty that made our little bit of money seem like so much to her. Later, I knew that we could never repay them for what they had done for us, but we tried by sending checks every month after we got to America. After their deaths, we continued to send checks for many years to Edek, their son, to make his life easier.

In my diary I even complained that my mother should have told me what it meant to find love and to carry a child and become a mother. I knew nothing. Then, I was young enough and spoiled enough to think she should have prepared me better. Stefka recognized my pregnancy before I did. Knowing what to expect would have made my first pregnancy and delivery easier; but, by that time, I was hiding in a tiny barn loft somewhere in Poland, and my mother was dying at Auschwitz. Not knowing what to expect from a pregnancy was nothing. My lasting and deepest regret is that my precious mother did not survive Auschwitz and would never be able to meet my beloved husband, or our children, or know the happiness Chaim and I had found together.

My diary also relates the times I felt I had reached the limit of my endurance, the times I wrote and cried to Chaim that I could take no more. Chaim never once felt we had reached the end of our endurance, the end of being able to survive in spite of overwhelming odds. He always thought we could find a way to keep going as long as we were together. He felt this so passionately that he convinced me too. We were strong enough to survive one more day, one more week, one more month, until better times came. Chaim knew in his heart we would reach freedom and live the normal life of our dreams.

Chaim's strength and courage, his tenderness and mental toughness, and his absolute refusal to consider defeat pulled me through. All the times I thought I could take no more, the times I begged to be allowed to die, to stop the suffering by going to sleep and not waking up, Chaim had enough determination for both of us. I could not have survived Sobibor, the escape, or what followed without my beloved Chaim by my side, holding my hand every step during our long and painful journey. Amazingly, Chaim said the same about my being by his side. I do sometimes admit that I had a few moments of courage too, because my Chaim was too smart to spend his whole life loving a weakling and a coward.

I will admit I am proud of having had the courage to refuse, in spite of being numb with fear, to give the names of people who had hidden me when I was arrested. I am also proud of stepping in front of Ulla at Sobibor when I thought one of the guards was going to harm her. Chaim gave me great credit for risking my life to steal food and for sharing it, but as I said earlier, I just had more places to hide food; and he was risking his life daily to steal what our lives would depend on when we escaped. I remember stepping in front of Chaim when we came across Polish escapees from Sobibor. They were going to shoot him if he didn't leave me behind and join them. It took more courage for me to walk five miles after my labor started to get help for the delivery of our first-born son, to survive a cruel, uncaring doctor who never touched me, and then to wait five days for Chaim to come take our son, Emielchen, and me home. Ann reminds me that I had the courage and the strength to survive months of brutal deprivation and then the death of our son, my mother's and brothers' deaths at Auschwitz and the loss of sixty family members at that and other camps. I only know I could not have survived any of it alone.

Chaim and I never knew how or why we experienced so many near death experiences and survived. Millions of others did not. We loved no more deeply, hoped no more passionately, prayed no more fervently than all the others. We knew then, and I know now, that our survival gave us the opportunity and the responsibility to speak for those whose voices were silenced. That responsibility continues to be overwhelming because of what and whom our story represents. The importance of our story, with its message of love defeating evil and of individual responsibility for creating a kinder, more tolerant world gave an enduring purpose to Chaim's and my life together. That same story and message now gives an enduring purpose to my life alone.

I have often wondered about the absence of help during the most terrible times in recorded history. Where were those who had the power to give aid while the ghettos and the camps were starving, brutalizing, and slaughtering thousands weekly? Did no one hear the stories? Did no one care? The questions no longer haunt my dreams nightly as they once did. To go on, I must eventually make peace even with what I can never hope to understand.

The comfort of thinking that the Holocaust was not stopped because no one knew what was happening is a dangerous lie and a denial of truth bought at a high price. I do know, in spite of protests to the contrary after the war, many Germans knew of Hitler's plans to rid Europe of all Jews and of the camps that executed those plans. Much of the world knew, and world leaders of major powers knew by 1942.

Pleading ignorance or denying the Holocaust, from the building of Dachau in 1933, to the Final Solution mandated in 1942, is also an insult to the thousands of people like Jan Karski, a Polish Catholic of high conscience, who risked his life to find the truth. Jan is one of many, but his stories were too extensive and well-documented to be ignored. Jan had heard rumors of forced deportations, transports, and mass exterminations;

but he knew that mere rumors would bring no aid from the rest of the world. He thought if he could get proof, the world would be forced to act. In his search for the truth, Jan had himself smuggled into the Warsaw Ghetto twice. Each time, he witnessed the same atrocities: mass starvation, stripped bodies lying in gutters, and members of Hitler's Youth on a *Judenjag* or 'Jew hunt,' shooting randomly and congratulating each other for each hit. His Underground guide kept repeating, "Remember this. Remember this." Jan would never be able to forget.

Soon after experiencing the Warsaw Ghetto, Jan bribed a Ukrainian guard to take him inside one of the concentration camps. Wearing a Ukrainian guard's uniform, Jan was smuggled into the holding camp in Izbica near Belzec and Lublin. He thought he was in one of the death camps, but discovered later that it was the last stop before prisoners were transported to one of the extermination camps.

At this holding camp, Jan witnessed brutality and horror on such a massive scale that he broke down physically and emotionally. Unable to continue, Jan had himself smuggled back out of the camp. He needed time to process what he had witnessed. He could not bear the reality of what he had seen thousands enduring. Time was needed for healing his mind and his soul. He didn't know if there was enough time for that kind of healing.

When Jan recovered, his mission to inform the world and to seek help intensified to the point of threatening his health. He felt he had to reach people who could stop the madness. He had to make them listen and act. Jan Karski carried his eyewitness accounts to the most powerful people in the world—to leaders in London, Washington, and the Vatican. Some found it impossible to believe that atrocities and mass murders were taking place on such a scale in the civilized world in the twentieth century. Some believed and were tormented by their inability to help. Many refused to acknowledge the truth of Jan's experiences. Time is needed to believe the unbelievable.

Those in power who believed everything Jan reported were grieved, but could offer no help. The Vatican sent word that they had done all they could do. The leaders of the Allied Forces felt that military operations could not be influenced by Jan's eyewitness accounts, no matter how painfully true or how carefully documented. The decision by the Allies was that the total focus of the war effort had to remain on the military defeat of Germany. They felt dividing efforts and resources would threaten eventual victory.

Jan continued trying to get something—anything—done that would stop or at least decrease the numbers being slaughtered, but nothing was done. Only symbolic resistance was evident as world powers promised that those responsible would not escape retribution when the war was over. The perpetuation of the greatest crime in human history was known but not stopped.

Years later, broken by his eyewitness reports failing to bring aid to the disappearing Jews of Europe, Jan would no longer describe the horrors he had seen. When asked, he would just repeat, "I saw terrible things."[41]

How many knew and how much was known? Was it easy to ignore what did not touch personally? Was failure to act based on heartless indifference or on political and military expediency? *Could* the world have stopped the mass murder of millions of men, women, and children? More questions with no answers. I think that too much of my life, maybe all life, is based on questions with no answers.

Chaim always warned that we must remember that Hitler didn't start big. He started small; and only because good people ignored his threat was he able to become an unquestioned tyrant. At first, he commanded no armies, he invaded no countries, he ordered no Final Solution. All who did not stand against him when he first began his march toward infamy allowed him to grow until no right-thinking person could support his insanity. By then, it was too late.

In spite of the danger, thousands voiced opposition and risked everything to resist the forces of evil. Resistance was mounted in multiple attempts on many levels. Often these attempts were futile, but occasionally some were successful in helping undermine Hitler's tyranny. Throughout German-occupied countries, ordinary people risked their lives to hide Jewish children and families. On more organized levels, thousands of young Jews and Partisans joined resistance movements or formed their own units. Underground groups grew in strength and with great courage supplied false documents and arranged escapes to neutral countries. Denmark helped most of its Jewish population transfer en masse to Sweden. Resistance increased as major uprisings took place in camps and ghettos. I am still proud of being part of the largest escape from any Nazi camp.

Three hundred of us said, "Enough! We will take no more!"

In April, 1943, prisoners in the Warsaw ghetto made the same decision. Against overwhelming odds, the last 60,000 surviving Jews, from a former population of 400,000, resisted a final deportation order and with almost no weapons held out for nearly a month against German tanks, armored cars, and flame throwers. The twentieth train on the way to Auschwitz was attacked, and 231 of the deportees escaped from the 1,600 aboard. Not one of the 231 who escaped was betrayed by the Belgians who hid them, in spite of Nazi threats.

How could millions have gone to their deaths without resisting? They didn't. They resisted in spite of the absolute power of the forces of evil, and the stories of their courage and resilience and heart are endless. History must continue to honor their courage and their memory.

During the brutal months in Sobibor and in hiding after the escape, I called on God many times. The world turned its back on us. God was not there, and I have yet to make peace with His absence. I know He was not at Sobibor, or Auschwitz, or Treblinka, or in the ghettos. I have not put Him on trial as others have done, but how could a merciful God not respond to the cries of the 6,000,000 Jews or the 11,000,000 total who perished before this embodiment of pure evil?

Ann and I have shared our ideas on faith as we have shared so many other thoughts. She feels that even when evil reigns supreme, God is there in every act of kindness, every instance of love shared, every courageous act of resistance. She reminds me of our survival and of the beautiful life Chaim and I shared. I repeat that God was not there for the mothers who prayed for the lives of their children to be spared, or for the faithful who entered the gas chamber in prayer, or for those whose suffering was so great that they prayed for a quick and merciful death. Ann and I seek and continue to find not necessarily agreement about God's presence, but always mutual caring, understanding, and respect. I hope this will be one of the results of all who share my story.

I did not want to live—and did not think I could live—without my Chaim. I still wish with all my heart that I did not have to, but I have learned that if I must, I can. I have learned to pay bills, write checks for Adam and Stefka's son, and hire help in the house and the yard for a few things I can no longer do. I still do all my own housework and most of the yard, but some of it is becoming too hard for me now. I have learned that I still enjoy reading *The New York Times* daily, being with my children, grandchildren and great-grandchildren, listening to good music, cooking and eating good food, and talking to friends, old and new. How I would love to share all those things with my beloved husband, but I have found the small joys in my life still exist, even without my Chaim beside me.

I marvel at the resilience of the human spirit, but I have no idea how to explain what can be endured and survived. Love?... Faith?... Hope?... Love cannot be destroyed. It exists in spite of everything man can do to destroy it. Faith took many to their deaths repeating, "Hear, O Israel, the Lord Our God, the Lord is One." Hope fills our hearts and minds and souls with the idea of the possible. How can man descend to such depths and rise to such great heights?

Even at my age or perhaps because of my years, I realize that there are no definitive answers for most of the truly important questions in life. It is, however, very important that we continue to ask them.

As painful as this remembering has been at times, it has also been joyful.

Dancing Through Darkness is my gift to the future for the love and the life Chaim and I shared. It is a gift from our past to help create a world where justice is determined by right, where the strong protect the weak, and where all who dare stand against injustice and cruelty are honored. My hope is that our story will inspire you to live your life so that you will be among those so honored.

"Thank you for taking the time to share my story."

— Selma Engel

Acknowledgments

Through the years of researching and writing this book, I have received amazing support from my family, from friends of many years, from recent acquaintances, and from strangers who became friends. My heartfelt gratitude goes to all for their help and unending patience.

Many years ago, God placed a dream in my heart of writing one life-affirming book and then placed the people in my life necessary to fulfill that dream. Harper Lee's *To Kill A Mockingbird* inspired, my mother's providing worthwhile reading and support enriched, and Selma's befriending and sharing her story made it possible. The list goes on, and if you have contributed and are not recognized, please forgive me. To all mentioned here and to those I neglected to mention, I can never repay you.

To Richard Rashke, author of *Escape from Sobibor,* for confirming the power of Chaim and Saartje's love story; Robert A. Croese of Croese Translation Services for deciphering words and meanings written in two languages in 1943, so Selma's diary could receive the place it deserves as part of The Holocaust Museum in Washington; Victor Judge of Vanderbilt University for his interest and encouragement; Danielle Kahane-Kaminsky, Executive Director of The Tennessee Holocaust Commission for her reading and approval; all members of The Writing Life, the Nashville Scribblers, the Session Class, and the Paperview Book Club for interest and support; Dennis Boswell and Joe Bruckner for research suggestions; Rudy Abramson, author, long time friend and mentor, who died before this book was finished, but whose example inspired even after his death; Jack and Donna Hurst, authors, who stepped in to continue professional advice after Rudy's death; Sherard Edington and Sue Parnell, current and former minister, who read and suggested needed changes; Charles Bradshaw, author, and his wife Loyce for readings and suggestions; Buddy Trouy for photo restoration; Jackie Pechin for graphic design and layout;

Anne Donnell, Emily Prather, and Kate Myers Hanson, author, for readings, suggestions, and invaluable editing services.

To my family for all the love, support, and joy you have always given me: Martha Walsh, Tom Walsh, Matt Walsh and their families, Larry, Charlie and Jimmy; Barb, Alaina, and Ian; Tiffany, Sofie, James, and Justin; Brenda Gill, my sister and computer guru, and her husband, Gordon and their family, Byron, Katrina, Luke, and Ella Kate; Heather and Jeff Livingston, Addy, and Markham; and Pauline Wiginton, my aunt, a source of wisdom and inspiration.

And finally to Selma Engel (Saartje Wijnberg) who welcomed me into her home with happy sheets and flowers for multiple week-long visits, shared her memories, no matter how painful the sharing became, encouraged me to use her memories and her diary as a basis for this book about a love strong enough to survive evil, and assured me after my first visit in 2006 that even if the book were never published, we had each found a new friend.

Notes

PART ONE
Chapter 2

1. Shirer, *The Rise and Fall of the Third Reich*, 135-149, hereafter referred to as *R&F*.

2. Hitler, *Mein Kampf*, 342.

3. Willmott, Cross, and Messenger, *World War II*, 17.

4. *R & F*, 95-96.

5. Ibid., 253.

6. Willmott, Cross, and Messenger, *World War II*, 18.

7. Sereny, *Into That Darkness, An Examination of Conscience*, 49-50.

8. Hitler, *Mein Kampf*, 302- 305.

9. Ibid., 361.

10. *R & F*, 965.

11. Ibid., 967-973.

12. Rashke, *Escape From Sobibor*, 52-53.

13. Hitler, *Mein Kampf,* 686.

PART TWO
Chapter 6

14. The Righteous

As Saartje Wijnberg and later as Selma Engel, Selma received life saving kindnesses from unexpected sources, as did thousands during that dark time in history. Others, who also number in the thousands, became their brothers' keepers to save as many as they could from the evil of the Third Reich. Often, the names of the Righteous have become legend: Oskar Schindler, who saved over 1000 Jews; the villagers of Le Chambon, France, a tiny Protestant farming village of 5000 who saved 5000 Jews; Irena Sendler who saved 2500 Jewish Children, the people of Denmark, who transported 8000 of their Jewish citizens to Sweden; and to over 22,000 other men and women from 45 countries who have been honored by Yad Vashem, the Holocaust Martyrs' and Heroes' Remembrance Authority as the Righteous among the Nations. These names are known and honored; many other names of people who risked their lives to protest evil and provide hope and sanctuary to fellow human beings may never be known.

PART THREE
Chapter 10

15. Selma Engel Interviews.

Chapter 12

16. *R & F,* 965-967.

17. Rashke, *Escape From Sobibor*, 10.

18. Ibid., 10.

19. Ibid., 12.

20. Ibid., 46.

Chapter 15

21. Sereny, *Into That Darkness*, 26-27.

22. Ibid., 48-49.

23. Ibid., 200-202.

24. Rashke, *Escape From Sobibor*, 24.

25. Ibid., 98.

PART FIVE
Chapter 20

26. *R & F*, 1008-1009.

27. Willmott, Cross, and Messenger, *World War II*, 150-151.

28. *R & F*, 1006.

29. Willmott, Cross, and Messenger, *World War II*, 182-183.

30. Berenbaum, The World Must Know, 183.

31. Sereny, *Into That Darkness*, 111.

32 . *R & F*, 967-974.

33. Ibid., 1037.

34. Ibid., 1038.

35. Ibid., 1041.

36. Willmott, Cross, and Messenger, *World War II*, 230-233.

37. *R & F*, 1086.

38. Willmott, Cross, and Messenger, *World War II*, 234-235.

39. *R & F*, 1095.

40. Ambrose, *Citizen Soldiers*, 461-464.

Chapter 28

41.Wood, Jankowski, Stanislaw, *Karski: How One Man Tried to Stop the Holocaust*, 72 ff.

Bibliography

Ambrose, Stephen E. *Citizen Soldiers*. New York: Simon & Schuster, 1997.

Arad, Yitzhak. *Belzec, Sobibor, Treblinka: The Operation Reinhard Death Camps*. Bloomington, Indiana: Indiana University Press, 1987.

Berenbaum, Michael. *The World Must Know: The History of the Holocaust as Told in The United States Holocaust Memorial Museum*. Boston, Toronto, London: Little, Brown and Company, 1993.

Blatt, Thomas Tiovi. *From the Ashes of Sobibor, A Story of Survival*. Evanston, Illinois: Northwestern University Press, 1997.

Dawidowicz, Lucy S. *The War Against the Jews: 1933-1945*. New York: Hold, Rinehart and Winston, 1975.

Elson, Robert T. *Prelude to War*. Alexandria, Virginia: Time Incorporated, 1976.

Fleming, Gerald. Hitler and The Final Solution. Los Angeles: University of California Press, 1982.

Green, Joshua M., Kumar, Shiva, ed. *Witness: Voices from the Holocaust*. New York: Simon & Schuster, 2000.

Gutman, Israel, editor-in-chief. *Encyclopedia of the Holocaust*. New York: Macmillen, 1990.

Hitler, Adolf. *Mein Kampf.* Vrlag Frz. Eher Nachf G.M.B.H. Munich, 1925. Boston: Houghton Mifflin Company, 1943.

Lipstadt, Deborah E. *Denying the Holocaust: The Growing Assault on Truth and Memory.* New York: Penguin Books, 1993.

Marks, Jane. *Hidden Children, The Secret Survivors of the Holocaust.* New York: Ballantine Books, 1993.

Mayer, Arno J. *Why Did the Heavens Not Darken? The Final Solution in History.* New York: Pantheon Books, 1988.

Mosley, Leonard. *On Borrowed Time: How World War II Began.* New York: Random House, 1969.

Rashke, Richard. *Escape From Sobibor.* Boston: Houghton Mifflin, 1982.

Sauvage, Pierre. *Weapons of the Spirit.* Los Angeles: The Chambon Foundation, 1989. Video Documentary, 90 minutes.

Schreiber, Marion. *The Twentieth Train: The True Story of the Ambush of The Death Train to Auschwitz.* New York: Grove Press, 2000.

Sereny, Gitta. *Into That Darkness: An Examination of Conscience.* New York: McGraw-Hill, Inc., 1974.

Sereny, Gitta. *Into That Darkness: From Mercy Killing to Mass Murder.* London: Andre Deutsch, 1976.

Shapell, Nathan. *Witness to the Truth.* New York: David McKay Company, Inc. 1974.

Shirer, William L. *The Rise and Fall of The Third Reich: A History of Nazi Germany*. New York: Simon and Schuster, 1960.

Suhl, Yuri. *They Fought Back: The Story of Jewish Resistance in Nazi Europe*. New York: Schocken Books, 1967.

United States Holocaust Memorial Museum. SHOAH Video Tapes of Chaim and Selma Engel: Reels 1 and 2, Washington, DC, 1993-94.

Velmans, Edith. *Edith's Story*. New York: Soho Press, 1999.

Wiesel, Ellie. *Night*. New York: Hill and Wang, 2006.

Willmott, H.P., Robin Cross, and Charles Messenger. *World War II*. New York: DK Publishing, 2007.

Wood, E. Thomas, Jankowski, Stanislaw M. *Karski: How One Man Tried to Stop the Holocaust*. New York: John Wiley and Sons, Inc., 1994.

Yad Vashem, The Holocaust Remembrance Authority. Israel, 1990.

Sources

Works cited in the Notes and the Bibliography were instrumental in providing historical background for Selma and Chaim Engel's story. No story can come to life without being supported by knowledge of people and events surrounding and in some instances creating the story.

Although the works cited helped create for me, and I hope for the reader, the world that Chaim and Selma had lived, loved, and survived in, the primary sources were multiple interviews, by phone and in person with Selma and with friends and family of the Engels.

Four week-long visits with Selma, from January 2006, through October 2011, allowed me to record her memories, get to know her as a person through contacts with friends and family, and take advantage of her extensive library on Jewish history and art. I wanted Selma and Chaim to exist first as real people whose love had helped them survive and live a normal life together for over sixty years, and then as historical figures caught up in one of the darkest periods of history.

In addition to sharing her memories and her books, Selma provided access to the SHOAH tapes recorded by each of them during the time Steven Spielberg was chairman of the Visual History Foundation, a comprehensive library of Holocaust testimonies. Richard Raske's book *Escape from Sobibor* and the movie by the same name based on the book were provided with comments about the actors and the experience of acting as consultants on the film. Albums and boxes of all family pictures and documents were made available to me as if I were a member of her family.

Ongoing contact with Selma by phone and letter continued throughout the writing and publishing of *Dancing Through Darkness* and will continue...as it always does with friends.

About the Author

Ann Markham Walsh is a former teacher and business owner whose love of writing life-affirming works has produced two plays, numerous essays and short stories, and three books.

Ann graduated from Vanderbilt University and attended The University of Edinburgh, Scotland.

To balance family and career, Ann established Walsh and Associates, which grew into an international training company, AMW International, specializing in customized training for major corporate clients.

Dancing Through Darkness is her first attempt at sharing her work by becoming a published writer. She is passionate about her faith, her family, her friends, helping those in need, exploring the world, and true stories that stand as living examples of selfless love being the only force powerful enough to defy and survive evil.

Ann lives on a farm in Lebanon, Tennessee, thirty miles from Nashville, and is working on a screen play of **Dancing Through Darkness** and her second book - **Vengeance Is ...**

Please contact us at www.amwalsh.com or annwalsh18@yahoo.com

Author's Note

The gift of acting as a conduit for this story has been, and will continue to be an amazing part of my journey. Introducing the story of two Holocaust death camp survivors whose love proved stronger than the consummate evil of the Third Reich has enriched, challenged, and disrupted my formerly peaceful existence, hopefully not forever. From the beginning, I have felt a responsibility for bringing the miracles of this story and its telling to as broad an audience as possible. Because our world desperately needs to be reminded of the existence of miracles and the power of love to birth hope and dreams, being part of such a reminder has been an enormous and overwhelming task.

When John Seigenthaler, creator and host of NPT's *A Word on Words* asked me how representing Selma's and Chaim's story felt, the only word that came to mind was "overwhelming." Remembering that Mark Twain said the difference between the right word and the almost right word is like the difference between lightning and the lightning bug, I maintain that "overwhelming" is exactly the right word.

The recorded memories of Selma Wijnberg Engel, her diary written in 1943, the stories of her husband of sixty years, Chaim Engel, and endless research of a period that is almost equal parts cruelty, courage, and sacrifice have combined to create a heightened level of awareness that seeks answers. Why was this allowed to happen? Could it have been prevented? How could a madman have convinced intelligent people to follow him? What kind of people could willingly be involved in the annihilation of millions based on one of the deadliest plans in modern history? Where was the public outcry, the voice of reason, of justice? Should a seemingly indifferent world share responsibility?

I would like to be able to tell you that I have found answers; the truth is that I have not. Research and interviews have given me mountains of information about this time; but I have not, and, I think, never will arrive at understanding. As the inhumane brutality of those times is beyond normal comprehension, it follows that questions and their answers may lead to more knowledge; but true understanding continues to elude us.

Since publication of the first edition of *Dancing Through Darkness* on March 1, 2013, and the book signings and presentations that followed, the reception by readers and audiences has been gratifying and humbling. The comments and questions from those who have read or heard this story of miracles have clarified multiple levels of meaning and led to a deeper understanding of what this story is meant to accomplish for this and future generations. Sharing a few of those comments and questions through these notes is an attempt to include those benefits for readers of this second edition.

Is Selma still living?

As of now (Fall, 2015), Selma is very much alive and doing as well as her ninety-three years will allow. I talk to her every two or three weeks, and occasionally her old sense of humor surfaces for a few minutes. More often than not, however, she tires quickly and asks me to call back the next day when she is sure she will feel better. She is now at an assisted living facility in Guilford, Connecticut, but insists she will be going home soon. I hope she can. She has beaten long odds before.

What have been the most common reactions to the book?

The most common reaction by far has been, "Thank you for doing this." When I made my fifth trip to Branford, Connecticut, to present Selma's book to her as a gift for her 91st birthday, the mantra for the day from family and friends was, "Thank you for doing this." And I rarely do a presentation that is not followed by those words or a similar thought from several members of the audience. From a fellow writer and university audience member, "Thank you for sharing a story that proves the power of love and hope to bring light from darkness."

The reaction that I hold closest to my heart was from an elderly gentleman in Georgia. He gave *Dancing Through Darkness* and me a sincere acknowledgment for bringing this story to as large an audience as possible. He stood close as I signed his book and said in a quiet, heavily-accented voice, "You are doing your part for Tikkun Olam." Not familiar with the words, I asked him to explain their meaning. "Tikkun Olam is Hebrew for healing or repairing the world. This story and the words you have spoken here tonight are a part of that healing. Thank you."

I hope his words are true. I don't know his name, but I think of him often and silently thank him for sharing his thoughts with me. I looked for him after signing other books and answering other questions, but with no luck. I still have no idea who he is, but his presence and his words honored and humbled me and continue to bless me and my work.

On a different level, an elderly woman in Michigan got nose to nose with me after the presentation and stated for all to hear. "You look really good for all you have been through." Her granddaughter quickly told her I was the author, not the subject of the book. At the other end of the spectrum in age and reaction was a fourth grader at Holy Rosary Academy in Donelson, Tennessee. She said that her school would have known what to do with Hitler because he was the biggest bully ever, and her school does not allow any bullying. She concluded with, "Down with Hitler! Up with pizza!" Somehow, from taking care of bullies and loving pizza to Tikkun Olam works for me.

The story as it is told to children is very different from the one for adult audiences, but the idea of individual responsibility for caring for each other and standing up for what is right is present in the notes their teachers have them write. I am touched by every one I read and astounded by their understanding and their heart.

Why was Selma willing to share their story with you?

When I first met Selma in 2007, she was still in deep grief over the death of Chaim. She had exhausted all possible listeners with her grief and her stories; that's why the first sentence for *Dancing Through Darkness* is, "Many will not want to know my story."

On the advice of family and friends, Selma had begun seeing a counselor to help lessen her grief over Chaim's death and move on with her life. "They tell me to carry on with my life. How can I? He was my life."

She wanted their story told as a way to honor their love and their life together and to warn of the dangers of ignoring evil until it becomes powerful enough to destroy everything in its path. Recording her memories was very difficult for her, but she was determined to see it through so their story would live as a part of their legacy instead of dying with her.

The other reason for her willingness to share their story is that from the first phone conversation, we had enjoyed talking and laughing together. We became friends and she trusted me. She gave her approval in writing of every section of the book as it was finished. She read it, or in one instance when she was sick for my whole visit, I read it to her.

I think our collaboration was meant to be as she told of a love strong enough to exist beyond its own time and place, and as such, I became the means of relating a story greater than any I could have imagined when I tore out Chaim Engel's obituary so many years ago.

Why did you choose this story as your first attempt at publication?

Actually, this story chose me. I can't explain it to you because I don't understand it, but I can tell you that from my tearing Chaim Engel's obituary from The Atlanta Journal-Constitution in 2003 until the 2013 publication date, everything and everyone I needed was there at exactly the right time. That doesn't mean the challenges or the difficulties disappeared, but I began to realize that this work was part of what I was supposed to do with my time on earth. Such a sense of vision and mission has a tremendously powerful effect,

When Victor Judge, Registrar of Vanderbilt Divinity School, told me that perhaps I had been born to tell this story, I initially disagreed. In retrospect, I may not agree that I was born just to tell this story, but I am willing to admit that this telling is a significant part of God's plan for my life.

My continuing mission – begun by Selma and Chaim – of speaking out against good people remaining silent in the presence of prejudice and injustice has been an unexpected but powerful addition to my God-given, childhood dream of doing life-affirming work.

You said in your presentation that you have always been a writer. Why did you write all those years if not for publication?

As a life-long lover of words and the worlds they create, my joy has always been in the process of putting words on paper. I have to write – that's how I process this complex and confusing but glorious world, how I savor the times of unlimited joy, and one way I connect with my Creator. Writing is as necessary for me as breathing, so much of my work over the years has paralleled what was going on in my life at the time. My writing clarifies, comforts, challenges, and reminds me constantly of how inextricably linked we all are. The commonalities of memory and an existence based on shared interdependence bind each of us to every other one of us.

What were the greatest challenges you faced in researching and writing this book?

Where do I begin? There were so many challenges, and each one seemed to open doors and invite others in. A few I had anticipated; most I had not. As I said earlier, whatever I needed to meet the challenges was always there.

The first challenge I faced was the feeling that I was inadequate for the task, that I lacked sufficient knowledge of this period in history or the experience needed for success in the unknown world of publishing. This feeling gradually disappeared as I became consumed by the beauty of the story and the historical research necessary to wrap it in the events of its time and place. There are many sayings that explain this phenomenon: "Take a leap of faith and His angels will catch you." This proved to be true, and I wonder if my angels, earthly and celestial, were as tired and as jubilant as I was by the time we finished.

Each day of research and/or writing began with two thoughts, one a line from Columbus' daily log, "Today we sail on." The other from Philippines 4:13, "I can do all things through Him who strengthens me." With these widely divergent thoughts leading me forward, I chained myself (mentally) to the yellow legal pad, the computer, the stacks of research materials, or all of the above. The moment I began, time and feelings of inadequacy ceased to exist. I would realize at the end of the day that I had missed lunch, but that I had created something that might be worthy of exercising Carson McCullers' adage to "revise, revise, revise."

A lot of reading and questioning were necessary for choosing resource materials; then came the challenges of using the historical research information to support the story without overwhelming it and determining how to separate the research from Selma's memories.

Friends offered to do the research for me, but I instinctively knew that this challenge I had to meet myself. The value of this decision to put in the grueling, but fascinating hours necessary cannot be overstated, not only for the outcome of the book, but for my personal growth. Online research was invaluable, but I still prefer voracious reading of books to get an all-round solid, in-depth feel for a subject.

Living vicariously in the midst of one of the most horrific times in history created another challenge, one that I had foolishly not anticipated.

Memories of brutality and suffering that I would choose to erase cling stubbornly and resurface when least expected. Unable to get rid of these memories completely, I have learned to focus on the selfless actions of courageous people who can provide enough hope for the human condition to somewhat lessen the power of darkness. After a while, I also learned to do the same thing Selma and I did when recording her memories became overwhelming – I remove myself physically, mentally, and emotionally until I can face it again.

Interesting detours in research created another challenge. Subjects surfaced that I had not anticipated, but felt compelled to explore because of my innate curiosity and their intrinsic value.

Deborah E. Lipstadts' work on Holocaust deniers and revisionists, *Denying the Holocaust, The Growing Assault on Truth,* opened the door to a world I had not known and had consequently underestimated. After reading her work, I was less disturbed than I would have been otherwise when I began receiving emails stating that what I had written never happened, it was all a lie, I had been duped, and the Jews were controlling America now as they had controlled Germany. The writers always offered to prove their facts if I was not afraid to respond and learn the truth. With anger and sadness that such virulent hatred could still exist, I quickly learned to use the immediate, albeit temporary, solution at my fingertips – delete, delete, delete.

Another worthy area was explored with Yuri Suhl's book, *They Fought Back: The Story of Jewish Resistance in Nazi Europe.* I had always wondered how so many could have gone to their deaths without resisting. They didn't. Stories of resistance, both individual and organized, put to rest any ideas I had about there having been so little. The resistance efforts were monumental and occasionally had a major impact; more often, the power of the Third Reich had reached such a stage of power and fear that resistance efforts proved futile in the face of the German War Machine. The effectiveness of the resistance efforts, or lack of, in no way diminishes the courage of those involved or the human dignity they inspired for those who had thought none was left to them.

Wood and Jankowski's work on Jan Karski, titled *Karski: How One Man Tried to Stop the Holocaust* is compelling enough for his story to be included in the final chapter of *Dancing Through Darkness.*

I had to try for an accurate and powerful portrayal of the times of unimaginable suffering from hunger, cold, and disease, the deprivation of a war-torn Europe that left them struggling for borderline survival, and the bottomless pit of grief that threatened Selma's will to live when Emielchen, their son and their hope for the future, died from spoiled milk. The horrors were real, the pain palpable, and unguarded moments meant sinking into a depressed malaise, or, even worse, being guilty of fostering a maudlin sentimentality that would dishonor what they had endured and survived. Neither choice was acceptable. I hope the balance was achieved sufficiently for readers to feel the horror of their deprivation and empathize with their pain but to realize even more strongly their courage and the power of their love: first as prisoners of the Nazi SS and guards at Sobibor Death Camp, after the escape as prisoners in the hayloft of Adam and Stefka's barnloft, and finally after the liberation as prisoners of the life-threatening conditions of post-war Europe. As Selma wrote in her diary on Sunday, August 13, 1944, "Is this the freedom we longed for? Oh, God, I can't take any more. I don't have the strength [illegible] I don't do anything but cry."

Balance for the brutal conditions of that time was created by their love as their hopes and dreams consistently rose above impossible circumstances to help them survive just one more day.

Do you feel Selma's memories of their experiences were reliable after so many years?

We know that memory is selective, but Selma's memories were as close to truth as memory can come. The recordings of our conversations, their individual SHOAH tapes, phone interviews with other survivors, and her diary were almost identical in relating the details of their lives. I never felt I was hearing other than the truth of those experiences. She did not tend to embellish or downplay, almost a "just the facts" manner, as evidenced by the recordings of our conversations. Her memories were vivid and full of detail, as if they had been locked away all those years and were just now being given a voice and the freedom to be heard.

When she began to talk of the past, her demeanor would change. Ordinarily verbally and facially expressive, when Selma talked of the past, she would become expressionless, almost robotic. I came to realize that her apparent detachment provided a fragile facade of protection that was necessary for her to relate any of their past, particularly the cruelest times. Even with the protection of allowing herself only to speak the memories, trying not to feel them, we would still became overwhelmed with this touching of the past and have to stop for the rest of the day or even skip a day. When necessary, we would leave the pain of the past and try to find comfort and peace in the present: planting her flowers, taking Sneakers for a walk, browsing nurseries, or visiting friends. We knew we would continue when we could, just not for a while.

If any of her memories had not rung true, I think her story would not have had the impact that it has had on me and on subsequent readers and audiences.

What did you gain from the experience?

More than I can fully describe, and I become more aware every day of how blessed I am to be a part of this experience. As I have said many times, it was a gift. The most significant benefits were the amazing people I met, with Selma, Chaim (through her words), and their friends and family at the top of the list, followed by rabbis, other writers, editors, publishers, readers, and audience members. All have been supportive, just pleased and grateful that I took the time, made the trips, and recorded a story that deserved to be remembered.

In addition to meeting people I would never have met otherwise, there is the sheer volume of knowledge gained from time spent immersed in this period. I often told friends that I sometimes felt my head would explode because I was filling it so full of new and often very detailed information.

The discipline required to complete this task was in itself a big plus. We only discover what we are capable of doing when we are pushed beyond what we thought we could do. My faith was strengthened every day because I could only do my part for that day without knowing the end result. I had to trust that what was supposed to happen to this story would if I just did my part. I was not in control of the outcome.

Difficult? Yes! The analogies that seem to fit the overall experience are hauling an elephant up Mt. Everest on my back with no oxygen supply, or more graphically, birthing my three children simultaneously without anesthetic. And I would not trade one minute of the experience in spite of the difficulties and the painful, sometimes impossible-to-erase memories.

I have always known what marvelous, mixed-bag creatures we are, but my faith in the resilience and generosity of the human spirit was justified over and over again by the selfless actions of ordinary people – if there is such a thing as an ordinary person. But on the other end of the spectrum is the heartache and despair over what human beings are capable of doing to each other over and over again.

What do you want your readers and audiences to gain?

I hope the book does for readers and audiences some of the same things it did for me.

I want each to realize anew the courage that exists on such an enormous scale in the most unlikely people and places, and that they resolve to honor all who were and are willing to risk their lives to ease the burdens of strangers.

I hope they realize that we are all capable of far more than we think and that we owe it to the world to explore our gifts and determine what each of us can do to help a kinder, more compassionate world evolve. Nelson Mandela said, "We do no one any favors by hiding our light and pretending to be smaller than we are" It takes the combined lights of many to shatter the darkness, and each of us carries a light within.

I hope they fall in love with the gentle man from Brudzew, Poland, and the feisty, funny young girl from Zwolle, Holland, but I also hope that they see beyond their story to the timeless power of love and hope and dreams for all people and all times.

I want them to become part of Tikkun Olam by being aware of how their words and actions can help repair our broken world. I want them to realize that courage and kindness on a small scale can have a huge cumulative, incremental impact.

I want them to gain greater empathy and tolerance for the other – more courage in standing up to evil, whether on a school bus, in a subway, at the office, or at a social gathering. I want them to be aware of the danger of any statement or action that denigrates another, regardless of perceived justification for the words, the looks, or the actions.

I want them to examine their personal values and expose any prejudices based on what a person was born to be.

That may be asking a great deal of one love story contained in a one small book. But I hope by now, you also believe in miracles.

Is there anything you would change about the experience?

Absolutely! I would love to have had the privilege of knowing Chaim Engel. His character and his courage have fascinated me from the beginning. Selma's loving words, descriptions by family and friends, and his SHOAH tapes left me with admiration, respect, and the impossible dream of knowing the man in person.

Originally, I thought that – because he was not present when I talked to Selma – I would have to work harder to show his heart and his brilliance. Actually, his character was such that he became as powerful in his absence as he would have been if he had been sitting at the kitchen table reading *The New York Times* while Selma and I talked.

Thank you once again for supporting *Dancing Through Darkness* and for taking the time to share the comments and questions from other readers and audiences. I hope your life is richer for the experience.

For all of us I wish:

L'Chaim, Shalom, and Chesed

Life, Peace, and the constant, enduring Love of God

Comments / Questions

_____

_____

_____

_____

_____

_____

_____

_____

_____

_____

_____

_____

Comments / Questions

_____

_____

_____

_____

_____

_____

_____

_____

_____

_____

_____